SOME BIBLE SCHOLARS HAVE SUGGESTED THAT IT WAS POSSIBLE THAT PAUL, LUKE, JAMES, PRISCILLA AND AQUILA, SILAS, APOLLOS, BARNABAS, OR CLEMENT OF ROME WROTE THE BOOK OF HEBREWS.

# THE EPISTLE TO THE HEBREWS

## WHO WROTE THE BOOK OF HEBREWS?

EDWARD D. ANDREWS

EDWARD D. ANDREWS

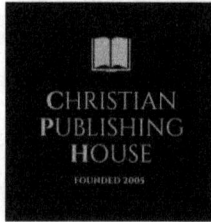

# THE EPISTLE TO THE HEBREWS

## Who Wrote the Book of Hebrews

Edward D. Andrews

CHRISTIAN PUBLISHING HOUSE
FOUNDED 2005

Christian Publishing House

Cambridge, Ohio

Christian Publishing House
Professional Conservative Christian
Publishing of the Good News!

CPH Since 2005

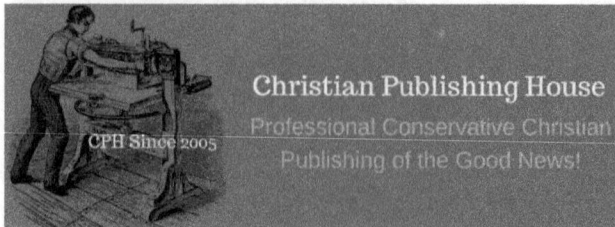

THE EPISTLE TO THE HEBREWS

Unless otherwise stated, Scripture quotations are from Updated American Standard Version (UASV) Copyright © 2020 by Christian Publishing House

*THE EPISTLE TO THE HEBREWS: Who Wrote the Book of Hebrews?* by Edward D. Andrews

ISBN-13: 978-1-949586-74-9

ISBN-10: 1-949586-74-X

EDWARD D. ANDREWS

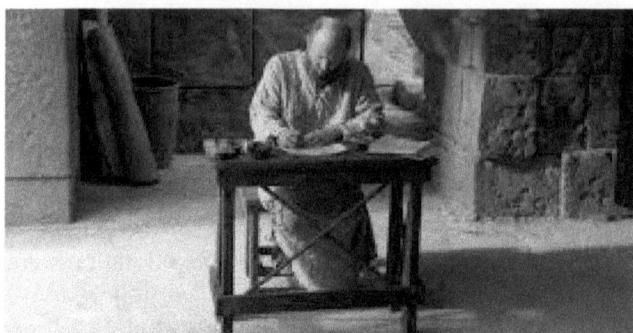

# Table of Contents

# THE EPISTLE TO THE HEBREWS

EDWARD D. ANDREWS

# Preface

Who wrote this important and enlightening book of Hebrews? Why does it really matter if the book is canonical, authoritative, and inspired? The book was not signed, and so there have been many suggestions over the centuries. Honestly, there is no absolute determinative evidence for any suggested author, even Paul. However, we do not live in an absolute world. God is absolute, and the Word of God in the original is absolute. It seems that most researchers that address this appear to offer just a few suggestions to live with the belief that it is best to say that we do not know. There have been many suggested authors since the first century: Paul, Luke, Barnabas, Silas, Apollos, Priscilla and Aquila, James, Philip, Jude, Clement of Rome have all been offered as suggested authors of the book of Hebrews. So, who really wrote the book of Hebrews? Indeed, the book of Hebrews is packed with the most relevant and beneficial information as well as with serious and weighty exhortation, excellent encouragement, and severe warnings lest we fall away from the faith. The better we become informed with this Bible book, the more we profit from what it has to say. Having some certainty as to who the author is will also give us a deeper appreciation of its authentic and authoritative state.

# Introduction

The apostle Paul was the accepted author of Hebrews for 1800 years. The new Bible scholar has served as the prosecutor, and the Christian apologist has served as the defense attorney. In many cases, the new Bible scholar has not offered enough to overrule the apostle Paul as the author of Hebrews. Since we are going to play out this quest for authorship of Hebrews as a though it was a court case, it should be noted that there are **three primary standards of proof**: **(1)** proof beyond a reasonable doubt, **(2)** a preponderance of the evidence and **(3)** clear and convincing evidence.

**NOTE:** The extras in the book about evidence, proof, Bible difficulties, and so on may not be 100% applicable to the question, 'who wrote the book of Hebrews,' but they will serve you well in other Biblical difficulties that you the reader will face. Therefore, look at all of the evidence for Pauline authorship and also ponder the extra material for what it is, how to approach, view, deal, explain the many hundreds of difficulties in the Bible.

Below we will use legal terms to define better how we should objectively view Bible evidence.

EDWARD D. ANDREWS

# CHAPTER 1 Legal Terms as to How We Should Objectively View Bible Evidence

**The burden of Proof:** The burden of proof falls on the one making the claims. If the Christian is witnessing to another, he has the responsibility to prove what he says is true, if he is asked for proof. However, if the critic is challenging the Christian, the burden of disproving lies with the critic. The closer the claim is to socially accepted knowledge, less proof is needed, while the further one moves from general knowledge, the more evidence is required. I believe that the legal burden of proof offers the best answers to the witnessing of others. Even with circumstantial evidence alone, a criminal can be convicted of capital murder, and receive the death penalty. Below we will list the levels of legal proof and some percentage and wording to indicate the degree of certainty needed. We have used different Bible objects for each one, but any criticism could be plugged into that particular burden of proof.

### Warrants Further Investigation

**Reasonable (30%):** This is a low-level burden of proof in that it is enough to accept something as *reasonably likely*, being so unless proven otherwise by a more in-depth look, which may bring in more evidence. For example, at this level, it is reasonably likely that Jesus Christ lived, died, and was resurrected. This may be achieved in the first conversation with the one with which we are sharing the good news.

**Probable (40%):** This is also a low-level burden of proof in that it is enough to accept something as *likely being so* unless proven otherwise by a more in-depth look, which may bring in more evidence. At this level, the Bible is probably the inspired, inerrant Word of God. This may be achieved in the first 2-3 conversations with the one with which we are sharing the good news.

### Conviction for Claim

**The preponderance of Evidence (51%):** This is a higher-level burden of proof that makes Noah surviving a worldwide flood *more likely to be true than not true.*

**Clear and Convincing Evidence (85%):** This is an even higher level of burden of proof that Adam and Eve were historical persons created by God is substantially *far more likely than not.*

**Beyond Reasonable Doubt (99%):** This is the highest level of burden of proof that over forty major prophecies about Jesus Christ in the Old Testament came true, being beyond a reasonable doubt. It must be understood that feeling as though we *have no reason to doubt* is not the same as 100 percent absolute evidence of certainty. If one has doubts that affect their belief of certainty, it is not beyond a reasonable doubt. This, too, must be qualified. It is reasonable **to have doubts about certain aspects of the whole,** as they may not have all the answers as of yet. However, it **does not affect the level of certainty as a whole.**

# CHAPTER 2 Defining and Dealing with Bible Difficulties

Bible critics be they atheists, agnostics, Muslims, and so on, want to tell us that there are mistakes, errors, and contradictions in the Bible. In fact, they would like us to believe that the Bible is filled with such things. They make this claim because they view the 40+ Bible authors as mere 'men writing the Bible.' However, we can reply, 'It is true. About 40+ imperfect men wrote 66 books over 1,600 years. But what you call mistakes, errors, or contradictions are actually Bible difficulties. What are Bible difficulties? They are difficulties that arise because the Old Testament 39 Bible books were written 3,500 years ago to 2,500 years ago in ancient Hebrew and Aramaic languages, within dozens of different ancient cultures. The New Testament 27 Bible books were written 2,000 years ago, over fifty years in the Koine Greek language, within many different ancient cultures. Thus, difficulties arise because we are from modern-day cultures thousands of years removed, translating, and interpreting ancient languages.

## Honestly

Whenever you find a difficulty in the Bible, frankly, acknowledge it. Do not try to obscure it. Do not try to dodge it. Look it square in the face. Admit it openly to whoever mentions it. If you cannot give a good, square, honest explanation, do not attempt any at all. Those, who in their zeal for the infallibility of the Bible, have attempted explanations of difficulties that do not commend themselves to the honest, fair-minded man, have done untold harm. People have concluded that if these are the best explanations; then, there are really no explanations at all. Thus, the Bible, instead of being helped, has been injured by the unintelligent zeal of foolish friends. If you are not really convinced that the Bible is the Word of God, you can far better afford to wait for a reasonable solution of a difficulty than you can afford to attempt a solution that is evasive and unsatisfactory.

## Humbly

Recognize the limitations of your own mind and knowledge, and do not for a moment, imagine that there is no solution just because you have found none. There is, in all probability, a straightforward answer, even when you can find no solution at all.

## Determinedly

Make up your mind that you will find the solution if you can through any amount of study and hard thinking. The difficulties of the Bible are our heavenly Father's challenge to us to set our brains to work. Do not give up searching for a solution because you cannot find it in five minutes or ten minutes. Ponder over it and work over it for days if necessary. The work will be more beneficial than the solution does. There is a solution somewhere, and you will find it if you will only search for it long enough and hard enough. Realize too that Christian apologists have given reasonable and rational answers for thousands of Bible difficulties, if a handful remains until the return of Christ, no harm is caused.

## Fearlessly

Do not be frightened when you find a challenging Bible difficulty, no matter how unanswerable or how insurmountable it appears at first sight. Thousands of men have encountered just such challenges, and still, the old Book has withstood the test of time, being the bestseller that will never be touched, in the untold billions of copies. The Bible that has stood eighteen centuries of rigid examination, and continuous and awful assault, is not likely to go down before your discoveries or before the discharges of any modern critical guns. To one who is at all familiar with the history of critical attacks on the Bible, the confidence of those contemporary critics who think they are going to annihilate the Bible, at last, is simply amusing.

# Patiently

Do not be discouraged because you do not solve every problem in a day. If some difficulty persistently defies your very best efforts at a solution, lay it aside for a while. Later it will likely be resolved, and you will wonder how you were ever perplexed by it.

# Scripturally

If you find difficulty in one part of the Bible, look for another scripture to throw light upon it and dissolve it. Nothing explains Scripture, like scripture. Repeatedly people have come to me with some difficulty in the Bible that had greatly staggered them and asked for a solution. I have been able to give a solution by simply asking them to read some other chapter and verse. The simple reading of that Scripture has thrown much light upon the passage in question that all the mists have disappeared, and the truth has shone as clear as day.

# Prayerfully

It is simply incredible how difficulties dissolve when one looks at them on his knees. Not only does God open our eyes in answer to prayer to behold wonderful things out of His law, but He also opens our eyes to look straight through a difficulty that seemed impenetrable before we prayed. One great reason why many modern Bible scholars have learned to be destructive critics is that they have forgotten how to pray.[1]

---

[1] All of this chapter except the initial paragraph is by R. A. Torrey. Edward D. Andrews has also enhanced Torrey's section as well.

# CHAPTER 3 A Few Relevant Basic Principles In Dealing with Bible Difficulties

## False or Mistaken Interpretations of the Bible

The Bible is filled with different genres, author intentions, among other things; therefore, imperfect humans are coming to the Bible with their 21st-century mindset and are going to go away with widely different interpretations frequently. Many of the difficulties that we encounter in the Bible are not from what is in the Bible itself, but rather from the unrealistic, mistaken, sometimes biased interpretation of the reader.

## Intended Meaning of Bible Author

The intent in criminal law is essential. First, the Bible student needs to understand the level that the Bible **intends to be exact** in what is written. What was the intent of the apostle Paul in Galatians and Luke in the book of Acts? Timothy George sums it up nicely, "Neither Acts nor Galatians was intended to be a day-by-day journal of Paul's activities ..."[2] Therefore, let's not treat Galatians-Acts like **a day-by-day journal,** nor have unrealistic expectations that Galatians-Acts will give us explicit evidence like **a day-by-day journal.** Neither Acts nor Galatians are a timetable for the life of the apostle Paul.

If Jim told a friend that 650 graduated with him from high school in 1984, it is not challenged, because it is all too clear that he is using rounded numbers and is not

---

[2] Timothy George, *Galatians,* vol. 30, The New American Commentary (Nashville: Broadman & Holman Publishers, 1994), 123.

meaning to be exactly precise. This is how God's Word operates, as well. Sometimes it means to be exact; at other times, it is merely rounding numbers, in other cases, the intention of the writer is a general reference, to give readers of that time and succeeding generations some perspective. Did Samuel, the author of judges, intend to author a book on the chronology of Judges, or was his focus on the falling away, oppression, and the rescue by a judge, repeatedly. Now, it would seem that Jeremiah, the author of 1 Kings was more interested in giving his readers an exact number of years.

**Acts 2:41** Updated American Standard Version (UASV)
⁴¹ So those who received his word were baptized, and there were added that day about three thousand souls.

As you can see here, numbers within the Bible are often used with approximations. This is a frequent practice even today in both written works and verbal conversations.

**Acts 7:2-3** Updated American Standard Version (UASV)
² And Stephen said:

"Brothers and fathers, hear me. The God of glory appeared to our father Abraham when he was in Mesopotamia, before he lived in Haran, ³ and said to him, 'Go out from your land and from your kindred and go into the land that I will show you.'

If you were to check the Hebrew Scriptures at Genesis 12:1, you would find that what is claimed to have been said by God to Abraham is not quoted word-for-word; it is simply a paraphrase. This is a normal practice within Scripture and in writing in general.

**Numbers 34:15** Updated American Standard Version (UASV)
¹⁵ The two and a half tribes have received their inheritance

beyond the Jordan opposite Jericho, eastward toward the sunrising."

Just as you would read in today's local newspaper, the Bible writer has written from the human standpoint, how it appeared to him. The Bible also speaks of "to the end of the earth" (Psalm 46:9), "from the four corners of the earth" (Isa 11:12), and "the four winds of the earth" (Revelation 7:1). These phrases are still used today.

## Unexplained Does Not mean Unexplainable

Considering that there are 31,173 verses in the Bible, encompassing 66 books written by about 40 writers, ranging from shepherds to kings, an army general, fishermen, tax collector, a physician and on and on, and being penned over 1,600 years, one does find a few hundred Bible difficulties (about one percent). However, 99 percent of those are explainable. Yet no one wants to be so arrogant to say that he can explain them all. It has nothing to do with the inadequacy of God's Word but is based on human understanding. In many cases, science or archaeology and the field of custom and culture of ancient peoples has helped explain difficulties in hundreds of passages. Therefore, there may be less than one percent left to be answered, yet our knowledge of God's Word continues to grow.

## Unrealistic Expectations Are Unhelpful Expectations

We should also note that **Unrealistic expectations** are unhelpful **expectations**. Even though it's challenging to set aside what we expect, hope, or desire a particular Bible book to tell us, work on relinquishing them unrealistic expectations because they can actually lead to doubt. And remember that God's Word of 39 OT books and 27 NT books, a total of 66 books are giving us exactly what we need to get through life or up unto the time of Christ's second coming. That understanding alone should actually inspire, support, and serve us well.

Remember (1) the intent of the Bible author is not meant to fulfill our expectations of what we want; the intention is to give the reader God's will and purposes. (2) A Bible book cannot be what it was not meant to be. An illustration of a book that is on the subject we might want, say a cookbook on cookies, yet after buying it, we find that it does not have the recipe for our favorite cookies. Yet, this does not mean the cookbook is worthless. A book on THE TEXT OF THE NEW TESTAMENT may come in the mail, and we might have been expecting an introductory level book. However, it ended up with an intermediate-advanced book, so do we go to Amazon and give a 1-star review, complaining about how the book was not what we wanted? Is that the author's fault that the customer had an unrealistic expectation, especially when the book description and the look-Inside-Feature made it clear what the intent of the author was?

# CHAPTER 4 Who Wrote the Book of Hebrews

Who is the author of the Book of Hebrews? Why does it really matter, if the book is canonical, authoritative, and inspired? The book was not signed, and so there have been many suggestions over the centuries. This book will provide evidence that the author of the book of Hebrews is, in fact, the Apostle Paul. Honestly, there is no absolute determinative evidence for any suggested author, even Paul. However, we do not live in an absolute world. God is absolute, and the Word of God in the original is absolute. It seems that most researchers that address this appear to offer just a few suggestions to live with the belief that it is best to say that we do not know. Having gotten that out of the way, I view biblical evidence like a criminal court views the level needed for a decision.

## Suggested Authors

There have been many suggested authors since the first century. James, Philip, and Jude have been offered as suggested authors of the book of Hebrews. Below is a short summary of evidence that is presented for some of the more common suggestions.

**Luke, as the Author:** The Greek of the book of Hebrews is literary Koine Greek, like what is found in the Gospel of Luke and the book of Acts. Luke had a long association with Timothy, who is mentioned twice in Hebrews. There are similarities with the doctrines of Paul. Luke was also a traveling companion of Paul.

**Barnabas, as the Author:** He was a traveling companion of Paul and a companion of Timothy. As was mentioned above, he was a Levite of the island of Cyprus

(Ac 4:36) and was a Hellenist; he was a Greek-speaking Jew.

**Silas, as the Author:** He was a traveling companion of Paul and a companion of Timothy. Many personal characteristics contribute to his name being offered. He was a Jew from Jerusalem, and well respected, and viewed as a prophet. (Acts 15:32) He played a major role in the circumcision issue in Antioch. (Acts 15:23)

**Apollos, as the Author:** The literary Koine Greek fits the training that he had received, he is from Alexandria, and the birthplace of the Septuagint (280-150 B.C.E.), and the Old Testament quotes from the book of Hebrews reflects his emphasis and the Septuagint. He was an eloquent speaker, with matches the eloquence of the book of Hebrews.

**Priscilla and Aquila as the Authors:** This view is supported by Adolf Harnack, who suggested Priscilla, because of her close ministry and working relationship with Paul. However, it really lacks in internal and external evidence. The fact that she is a woman would be reason enough to leave the letter anonymous.

**Clement of Rome as the Author:** (d. about 100 C.E.) There are a few similarities between the Book of Hebrews and the apocryphal book 1 Clement. (Heb. 11:7 and 1 Clem 9; Heb. 11:31 and 1 Clem 12; Heb. 1:3-13 and 1 Clem 36) In addition, there is a similarity in the way the two books cite Scripture. (Heb. 2:6; 4:4 and 1 Clem 15; 21) Then, there are the similarities of: connecting multiple Scripture quotations together, the similarity in the flow of argument, and the movement from example to the application.

Up until the 1800s, the most recognized suggested author was the Apostle Paul. In 1930, there was a discovery of the Chester Beatty P[46] (papyrus No. 46), which had been copied (150 C.E.), about 100 years after the death of the Apostle Paul. (Comfort and Barret 2001, pp. 203-06) P46 contains Hebrews among nine of Paul's letters, coming after Romans. The early church unanimously viewed Paul as the author. Pantaenus, who ran the Catechetical School in Alexandria around 180 C.E., accepted Paul as the author. This holds true of both his successors: Clement of Alexandria (150-215 C.E.) and Origen (184-254 C.E.). It should be mentioned that the Western church doubted that Paul was the author. It was Jerome and Augustine who accepted the authorship of Paul, which contributed to the West eventually accepting it as well. Thus, Hebrews is listed among "fourteen letters of Paul the apostle" in "*The Canon of Athanasius*," of the fourth-century C.E.

## Excursus on Origen

Origen is the most noted early scholar of Alexandria, Egypt. Concerning the authorship of Hebrews, many commentaries quote him out of context. They do not even reflect the whole of his comment if their quote was accurate. For example, Dr. George H. Guthrie in his NIV Application Commentary on Hebrews writes, "With Origen we confess our ignorance: 'Who wrote the epistle, God only knows the truth.'" (G. H. Guthrie 1998, p. 27) Let us say for the sake of argument that Origen was referring to the author of Hebrews. What Guthrie leaves out is that just before that statement, Origen writes, "If then, any church considers this epistle as coming from Paul, let it be commended for this, for neither did those ancient men deliver it as such without cause." (Cruse 1998, 6.25.13-14, p. 216) Also, Origen quoted from the book of Hebrews over 200 times as being Paul's epistle. It is a bit disingenuous to quote the small phrase of Origen, and not include the fact that Origen "accepted Pauline authorship," and "consistently quoted Hebrews as Paul's and commended those Churches that held to the Pauline authorship." (Lea 1999, p. 496) Worse still, Origen was quoted out of context, as the quote, "Who wrote the epistle, God only knows the truth," was not meant for the author of Hebrews, it was uncertainty about the scribe that took down the letter to the Hebrews as Paul spoke.

# The Grouping of Certain Books

First, it must be understood that the synoptic Gospels were published orally for many years before the written text came to market. With many of the writers of the Christian Greek Scriptures, you have the author himself penning the book (rough draft), making needed corrections, and then producing the 'authorized' text. From this authorized text, other copies were made. For those authors who dictated their writings, the scribe would take it down initially in shorthand and then create a rough draft to be corrected by the author and himself. From this, the scribe would produce the authorized text for the author to sign in his own hand. After the individual books had been in circulation for a few decades, the community of Christians throughout the Roman Empire started to form collections, such as combined books of the Gospels, and compilations of the Apostle Paul's letters. These groupings were accomplished by 125 C.E., with the total collection of the 27 books of the Christian Greek Scriptures coming together by 325 C.E. There is no doubt that throughout this process of publishing, copying, collecting, and canonizing of the Christian Greek Scriptures, those involved recognized these writings as being authoritative, no less than the graphē [Scriptures] of the Hebrew Old Testament books.

In other words, toward the close of the first century, Christians were gathering certain New Testament books together and dispensing them as a collection. The first to be collected might have been the four Gospels and then the Gospels and Acts. However, the letters of the Apostle Paul are even more likely to have been first. These groupings were available by the early part of the second century, and again we have P[46], which dates to 150 C.E., and just so happens to be a collection of Paul's letters, and included the books of Hebrews in the prominent position, right after Romans.

**2 Timothy 4:13** Updated American Standard Version (UASV)
[13] When you come, bring the cloak that I left behind in Troas with Carpus, and the scrolls,[3] especially the parchments.[4]

In not so many words, the apostle Paul urged his fellow traveling companion Timothy to bring him different types of written material. What did Paul mean by the scrolls and parchments? Textual scholar Philip Comfort offers us three options here,

> In Paul's final epistle (2 Timothy), he gives a directive to Timothy that gives us some insight into what kind of writing materials he was using. He told Timothy to bring to him *ta biblia malista tas membranas*. This has been interpreted in various ways, three of which are quite significant:
>
> 1. Paul was asking for "the scrolls" (presumably copies of Old Testament books) and "the parchment codices" (presumably copies of various New Testament books—perhaps of Paul's epistles or the Gospels).
>
> 2. Paul was asking for "the books" (presumably copies of Old Testament and New Testament books) *and* "the parchments" (perhaps blank writing material or notebooks containing rough drafts).

---

[3] Lit *little books*; (Gr. *biblia*) scrolls of Old Testament Scripture

[4] Lit *the parchments* (Gr. *biblia, membranas*) notes or letters of some type in codex form

Both of these interpretations understand that Paul was asking for two different kinds of documents. But another interpretation (espoused by Skeat) posits that *malista tas membranas* is a further definition of *ta biblia* because *malista* has a particularizing function. Thus, the third interpretation:

3. Paul was asking for "his books—that is, his parchment notebooks" (which were codices—note the term *membranas*).

If this third interpretation is correct, it suggests that Paul was anxious to get some of his written notes or rough drafts he had left behind when he was arrested. Since he could have secured Old Testament writings from various sources, it stands to reason that he would have been anxious to have his collection of epistles and/or his writings not yet published. Of course, this is conjectural. This much we can be sure of: Paul was using codices, whether in completed book form or in notebook form. And since Paul himself made mention of codices, it stands to reason that Paul's epistles were the first to be collected into codex form.[5]

By 65 C.E. when the apostle Paul wrote these words to Timothy, we have the canonical 39 books of the Hebrew Old Testament, which had been listed by either 22 books or 24 books (by combining certain books together as one), most of these were in separate scrolls because scrolls were rolled up and usually only written on one side. Professor Alan Millard said if such scrolls, "a price of six to ten denarii [six to ten days wages] for a copy of Isaiah. While this is no cheap, it would not put books out of the reach of the reasonably well-to-do." (Reading and Writing in the Time of Jesus (2001, p. 165) | Aug 1, 2000) Some had access to these OT scrolls. For example, in the

---

[5] hilip Comfort, *Encountering the Manuscripts: An Introduction to New Testament Paleography & Textual Criticism* (Nashville, TN: Broadman & Holman, 2005), 29.

book of Acts, we find the Ethiopian eunuch, who was "seated in his chariot, and he was reading the prophet Isaiah." He was "a court official of Candace, queen of the Ethiopians, who was in charge of all her treasure. He had come to Jerusalem to worship." Clearly, he was wealthy enough to have access to the book of Isaiah. – Acts 8:27-28.

Once more, Paul requested of Timothy: "When you come, bring the cloak that I left behind in Troas with Carpus, and the scrolls, especially the parchments." (2 Tim. 4:13) What we learn from this is that Paul who carried out his missionary work on very little, yet he owned a number of books. His library was the Word of God! Looking again at the word "parchments" in this verse, paleographer (papyrologist) scholar A. T. Robertson observed: "These in particular would likely be copies of Old Testament books, parchment being more expensive than papyrus, possibly even copies of Christ's sayings (Luke 1:1–4)." (A.T. Robertson, Word Pictures in the New Testament (Nashville, TN: Broadman Press, 1933), 2 Ti 4:13.) "Scrolls" literally referred to *little books*; (Gr. *biblia*) scrolls of Old Testament Scripture, while "parchments" (Gr. *biblia, membranas*) were notes or letters of some type in codex form. It is as Comfort said above, the apostle "Paul's epistles were the first to be collected into codex form." Too, we must remember that the apostle Paul from his you up until his encounter with Christ was **educated at the feet of Gamaliel** according to the strict manner of the law of [his] fathers, being zealous for God as all of you are this day." Yes, Paul was taught by a world-renowned Jewish teacher of his day, "a Pharisee in the council named Gamaliel, a teacher of the law held in honor by all the people." Therefore, we can understand how he came to have his own personal copies of the scrolls of God's Word. – Acts 5:34; 22:3.

# Christians' Use of Scrolls

Even so, leave no doubt in your mind, for any Christian or Christian congregation for that matter to possess any of Scripture, be it Old Testament books, Paul's letters, the Gospels, and so on, it would have been a privilege in the extreme. Many of the Christians in the early days had access to the Scriptures of the Old Testament because for the first seven years, from 29-36 C.E., all those coming to Christ were only Jewish converts. With many of the Christian congregations by 65 C.E. having a large foundation of Jewish Christians, we note Paul's earlier letter to Timothy, "Until I come, devote yourself to the public reading of Scripture, to exhortation, to teaching." (1 Tim. 4:13) Public reading within the Christian congregation was carried over from the practice of public reading that had gone on in the Jewish synagogues. Public reading was a practice that had been a part of the lives of God's people since the days of Moses. – Acts 13:15; 15:21; 2 Corinthians 3:15.

# Doctrinal and Stylistic Similarities Between Paul and Hebrews

1. The book of Hebrews begins with Jesus Christ's work in creation, as does the book of Colossians. (Heb. 1:2; Col 1:16)

2. Jesus took on the form of his brothers, to be like them in every respect, as he suffered in his ransom sacrifice. (Heb. 2:14-17; Phil 2:5-8)

3. Christ mediates and new and better covenant. (Heb. 8:6; 2 Cor. 3:4-11)

4. The gifts that were given by way of the Holy Spirit. (Heb. 2:4; 1 Cor. 12:11)

5.  The warning example of unbelief to the Hebrews from the Israelite history. (Heb. 3:7-11; 4:6-11; 1 Cor. 10:1-11)

6.  The similarity of a request that the readers pray for Paul and his work. (Heb. 13:18;Rom 15:30)

7.  "Now may the God of peace," is exact. (Heb. 13:20; 1 Thess. 5:23)

8.  "Our brother Timothy" is similar to four of Paul's other letters. (Heb. 13:23; 2 Cor. 1:1, Col 1:1, I Thess. 3:2; Phm. 1)

9.  Paul's letters to the Philippians, the Colossians, and Philemon, were written from Rome, as Paul was imprisoned, and Timothy was at his side. This circumstance fits the circumstances of the closing of Hebrews. (Heb. 13:23-24; Php 1:1; 2:19; Col 1:1, 2; Phm 1)[6]

10. Paul's trademark ending "be with all of you," is found in Hebrews and a number of Paul's letters, whether it be 'grace' or 'peace' or 'love' or 'holy Spirit,' or 'the Lord' or Jesus Christ' "be with all of you." (Heb. 13:25; Rom. 15:33; 1 Cor. 16:24; 2 Cor. 13:14; 2 Thess. 3:16, 18; Tit 3:15)

11. When we look at the textual evidence, the evidence points to ending in the manuscripts of the autographs were much shorter. For example, Philemon would have ended with "grace be with you," rather than the longer ending, "grace of our Lord Jesus Christ be with your spirit. Amen."

---

[6] It should be noted that this is Paul's first imprisonment (59 to 61 C.E.), and Timothy, a very close traveling companion of Paul for some 15 years is mentioned twice. Timothy could have served as served as Paul's amanuensis, the person to write from Paul's dictation of what would become the book of Hebrews.

## Hebrews and Paul's Other Writings

| Hebrews 1:3 | Colossians 1:15 – 17 |
|---|---|
| "The Son is the radiance of God's glory and the exact representation of his being, sustaining all things by his powerful word." | "The Son is the image of the invisible God. . . . For in him all things were created . . . and in him all things hold together." |
| **Hebrews 2:4** | **1 Corinthians 12:11** |
| "God also testified to it by signs, wonders and various miracles, and by gifts of the Holy Spirit distributed according to his will." | "All these are the work of one and the same Spirit, and he distributes them to each one, just as he determines." |
| **Hebrews 2:14 (–17)** | **Philippians 2:7 – 8** |
| "Since the children have flesh and blood, he too shared in their humanity so that by his death he might break the power of him who holds the power of death. . . ." | "Being made in human likeness. And being found in appearance as a human being,<br><br>he humbled himself<br><br>by becoming obedient to death —<br><br>even death on a cross!" |
| **Hebrews 8:6** | **2 Corinthians 3:6** |
| "But in fact the ministry Jesus has received is as superior to theirs as the covenant of which he is mediator is superior to the old one, since the new | "He has made us competent as ministers of a new covenant — not of the letter but of the Spirit; for the letter kills, but the Spirit gives life." |

| | |
|---|---|
| covenant is established on better promises." | |
| **Hebrews 10:14** | **Romans 5:9; 12:1** |
| "For by one sacrifice he has made perfect forever those who are being made holy." | "Since we have now been justified by his blood"; "offer your bodies as a living sacrifice, holy and pleasing to God." |

# Differences Between Paul and Hebrews

1. The book of Hebrews is anonymous, whereas no other writing of Paul is anonymous. Sometimes we are quick to dismiss exceptions to the rule, this lack of clear proof of identity of the writer would clearly not rule out Paul. If there is a reasonable reason for the omission of the name, and other evidence supports Paul, let us leave it at that. Other New Testament books do not name the author, who is then identified by internal evidence and external support. Some have logically suggested that Paul intentionally omitted his name, as the letter was to go to the Hebrew Christians in Judea, and his name was greatly hated by the Jews there, and the Hebrew Christians were under stress from them as it was. (Acts 21:28)

2. Hebrews 2:3: "how shall we escape if we neglect such a great salvation? It was declared at first by the Lord, and it was attested to us by those who heard." This verse has cause most to suggest that if Paul were the author of Hebrews, it would conflict with his words at Galatians 1:1, 11-12, where he states that he received the Gospel

29

through Jesus Christ. However, Hebrews 2:3 seems to suggest that the author is a second generation Christian, having been taught the Gospel by others who had heard it. However, the context seems to suggest otherwise. It seems that Paul is merely stating here that he did not receive the Gospel during Jesus' three and half year ministry here on earth, like the others.

3. It is a fact that the Greek in most of Paul's letters is more of a conversational Koine; Hebrews is more of a literary Koine. This could be a simple case of different settings and audiences requiring different levels of writing. There is likely no scholar that would ever suggest that Paul could not write in the literary Koine. (1 Cor. 13)

4. Jesus is the great high priest of the book of Hebrews, which is not to be found in Paul's other writings. This logical fallacy is known as an argument from silence, an assumption drawn-out based on the lack of evidence, as opposed the presence of evidence. Again, different setting, require different subject matter.

## The canonicity of the Book of Hebrews

What is the Bible canon, and how did this term come about? What are some of the aspects that are used to determine a book's canonicity?

The English word "canon" goes back to the Greek word kanon and then to the Hebrew qaneh. Its basic meaning is "reed," our English word "cane" being derived from it. Since a reed was sometimes used as a measuring rod, the word kanon came to mean a standard or rule. It was also used to refer to a list or index and when so applied to the Bible denotes the list of books which are received as Holy Scripture. Thus if one speaks of "canonical" writings, one is speaking of those books which are regarded as having divine authority and which comprise our Bible. (Lightfoot 1963, 1988, 2003, p. 152)

Before reading the rest of this paragraph, ponder and consider this question: how many books of the New Testament were written by Archippus, Claudia, Damaris, Linus, Persis, Pudens, and Sopater? None right? Why? All of those mentioned were traveling companions of the Apostle Paul. However, Paul had over 100 traveling companions. These were some of the most unfamiliar, because they received little press in the New Testament, and were unknown to most of the New Testament world at that time. Using a modern day example, if I were to ask, 'who knows Pastor Rodney Uhlig?' While he too is a person that would have been willing and qualified to travel with someone like the Apostle Paul, you do not know him, as he is mostly known to his local community and congregation. However, what if I were to ask, 'who is Reverend Billy Graham,' would you know him? Most of the world would know who he is. There are a lot of aspects that signal a book of the Bible as canonical. However, we are going to focus our attention on one criterion. "Every New Testament book was written by an apostle or prophet. Thus each book has either apostolic authorship or apostolic teaching."[7]

All of the writers of the Greek New Testament somehow or other were closely affiliated with the Jerusalem Council (Acts 15:1–35), which was made up of apostles personally selected by Jesus, Jesus' half-brother and elders. Matthew, John, and Peter were of the original twelve apostles. The apostle Paul, while he was an apostle, though not of the twelve, he was specifically selected by Jesus after Jesus had ascended to heaven. James, Jude (half-brother of Jesus), and Mark were at the outpouring

---

[7] Norman L. Geisler and William E. Nix, A General Introduction to the Bible, Rev. and expanded. (Chicago: Moody Press, 1996), 212.

of Holy Spirit at Pentecost. (Acts 1:14) Peter clearly reckons the letters of Paul in with "the other Scriptures." (2 Pet. 3:15, 16) Both Mark and Luke were friends and traveling companions of the Apostle Paul, as well as Peter. (Acts 12:25; 1 Pet. 5:13; Col. 4:14; 2 Tim. 4:11) In fact, the Gospel of Mark is recognized as being from both Peter and Mark: Peter's account, Mark penning it. "That relationship notwithstanding, Mark had his own God-given ministry (Acts 12:25; 2 Tim. 4:11)." (Geisler and Nix 1996, p. 212-13) Each of these writers had received Holy Spirit, at either Pentecost on the road to Damascus (Acts 9:17, 18), or by the laying of hands by the apostles. (Acts 8:14-17) All of these writers were well-known in the first century Christian congregation.

Within the Old Testament, we see that the books were written by persons that were known to all of Israel: such as Moses, Joshua, David, Isaiah, Jeremiah, Ezra and Nehemiah. "In the New Testament as well as the Old, the determining factor in whether a book was canonical was its propheticity." (Geisler and Nix 1996, p. 212) If we read Deuteronomy 13:1-8, where Moses sets out the criteria of a prophet, we see that he was a man of signs and wonders, as well as a proclaimer of God's Word. Whether the people of God were the Israelites or the first-century Christian congregation, they accepted the proclamations from men who possessed supernatural gifts as the inspired Word of God

More so, in the New Testament era, the apostle filled the office of prophet (a proclaimer of the gospel) as well. At Acts 1:21-22, Peter informs us as to the qualifications to be an apostle; it must be "one of the men who has accompanied us during all the time that the Lord Jesus went in and out among us, beginning from the baptism of John until the day when he was taken up from us, one of these men must become with us a witness to his resurrection." Of course, this criterion was to fill the position of one of the twelve apostles. The Apostle Paul was not one of the twelve, but he was handpicked specifically by Jesus himself. This apostle has penned 13 books, half of the New Testament books. If you accept that he penned Hebrews, as this writer does, then he has penned over half. At 2 Corinthians, Paul tells us that "the signs of a true apostle were performed among you with utmost patience, with signs and wonders and mighty works." If a person was not appointed, had not seen Christ, or had not evidenced his office with signs or miracles, his claims would have been unacceptable. "Every New Testament book was written by an apostle or prophet." (Geisler and Nix 1996, p. 212)

## In Conclusion

Is there absolute certainty that the Apostle Paul wrote the book of Hebrews? No. We cannot place absolute certainty on it, and it is unfair to take this one book and suggest that this is the criterion that we need. Based on the evidence above, is it fairly likely that Paul wrote the book of Hebrews? Yes, so we can say that it is reasonably so. Can we say that it is fairly likely that Luke, Clement of Rome, Apollos, or another wrote the book of Hebrews? Yes, it is reasonable. What about the level of being probable, is it likely for either Paul or any of the other recommendations? Yes, it is probable. Can we say that it is more likely to be true than not true that Paul or any of the other recommendations wrote the book of Hebrews? Yes for Paul, but a few of the other recommended writers would fall off at this point, such as Clement of Rome, Luke, Silas and Priscilla and Aquila.

Is the evidence clear and convincing that Paul wrote the book of Hebrews, being substantially more likely than not? Yes. What about the others who are still in the running at this level of certainty? There are those that would argue that Barnabas and Apollos are serious candidates, and would be retained at this level of certainty.

I would not. I personally believe that when weighed, the evidence points to the Apostle Paul as being beyond a reasonable doubt. Is it absolute evidence of certainty? No. However, some issues that can be raised are not really issues at all, when they are looked at more deeply. Regardless, it is acceptable to have concerns about certain aspects of the whole, yet this does not affect the certainty of the whole. Therefore, for this writer, it is beyond a reasonable doubt that the Apostle Paul did pen the book of Hebrews. Am I at odds with most of the scholarship today? Yes. However, the majority of anything is not right merely because they are the majority.

Daniel Wallace gives us, "The arguments against Pauline authorship, however, are conclusive: (1) this letter is anonymous (or at least lacks the author's name on the *recto* side of the papyrus scroll), which goes contrary to the practice in all of Paul's canonical letters; (2) the style of writing is dramatically better than that of Paul (though an amanuensis could have been used); (3) the logical development is much more tightly woven than is Paul's (could an amanuensis have altered the core of the argument?); (4) the spiritual eyewitnesses are appealed to, while Paul insisted on no intermediaries for his gospel (cf. Gal. 1:12); and (5) Timothy's imprisonment (Hebrews 13:23) simply does not seem able to fit within Paul's lifetime, since he is mentioned repeatedly both in Acts and in Paul's letters and always as a free man." – Bible.org

## A Simple Review of Some of the Evidence

1. The Chester Beatty Papyrus P46 c. 200 C.E. contains a collection of Paul's epistles and includes Hebrews.

2. The stylistic differences from Paul's other letters are attributed to his using a scribe and the subject matter and the audience being different (a Jewish

viewpoint, designed to appeal to the strictly Hebrew readers).

3. It is Pauline because it certainly does have a Pauline character, which (which even Origen admitted).

4. Its obvious literary and theological depth leans toward Paul.

5. The epistle closes in a typically Pauline fashion (13:25). Hebrews closes with "Grace...be with you..." as he stated explicitly in 2 Thess. 3:17-18 and as implied in 1 Cor. 16:21- 24 and Col. 4:18. This closing greeting is found at the end of each of Paul's letters.

6. Timothy is associated with the author (13:23)

7. Daniel Wallace, who strongly believes it not to be Paul, admits "the macro-structure of the epistle is similar to Paul's style (doctrinal, followed by practical portion); and (4) there are several strong hints both of Paul's point of view and even his wording in this letter (especially when compared to Galatians)"

8. The style of writing in the book of Hebrews is far better (classical in style) than Paul but this could be because of his audience and that he used a scribe. Moreover, Paul had a classical education under Gamaliel, so my take is that he held back in his own knowledge, and he was capable of far more complex Greek than he normally displayed in his other thirteen letters. He was humble in his writings.

9. The letter being anonymous is because of the audience, as Eusebius says that Paul omitted his name because he, the Apostle to the Gentiles, and was writing to the Jews.

10. The author was not one of the twelve apostles. (2:3-4) (Paul Luke, James, Apollos, and Barnabas fit this)

11. He wrote before Jerusalem was destroyed (7-8) (Paul Luke, James, Apollos, and Barnabas fit this)

12. He knew the Old Testament very well, 98 citations. (Paul Luke, James, Apollos, and Barnabas fit this)

# APPENDIX I Bible Difficulties Explained

IT SEEMS THAT the charge that the Bible contradicts itself has been made more and more in the last 20 years. Generally, those making such claims are merely repeating what they have heard because most have not even read the Bible, let alone done an in-depth study of it. I do not wish, however, to set aside all concerns as though they have no merit. There are many who raise legitimate questions that seem, on the surface anyway, to be about well-founded contradiction. Sadly, these issues have caused many to lose their faith in God's Word, the Bible. The purpose of this books is, to help its readers to be able to defend the Bible against Bible critics (1 Pet. 3:15), to contend for the faith (Jude 1:3), and help those, who have begun to doubt. – Jude 1:22-23.

Before we begin explaining things, let us jump right in, getting our feet wet, and deal with two major Bible difficulties, so we can see that there are reasonable, logical answers. After that, we will delve deeper into explaining Bible difficulties.

### Is God permitting Human Sacrifice?

**Judges 11:29-34, 37-40?** Updated American Standard Version (UASV)

[29] Then the Spirit of the Lord was upon Jephthah, and he passed through Gilead and Manasseh; and passed on to Mizpah of Gilead, and from Mizpah of Gilead he passed on to the sons of Ammon. [30] And Jephthah **made a vow** to Jehovah and said, "If You will indeed give the sons of Ammon into my hand, [31] then it shall be that **whatever** comes out of the doors of my house to meet me when I return in peace from the sons of Ammon, it shall be Jehovah's, and I will offer it up as a burnt offering." [32] So

Jephthah crossed over to the sons of Ammon to fight against them; and Jehovah gave them into his hand. <sup>33</sup> He struck them with a very great slaughter from Aroer as far as Minnith, twenty cities, and as far as Abel-keramim. So the sons of Ammon were subdued before the sons of Israel.

<sup>34</sup> When Jephthah came to his house at Mizpah, behold, **his daughter was coming out to meet him** with tambourines and with dancing. Now she was his one and only child; besides her he had no son or daughter.

<sup>37</sup> And she said to her father, "Let this thing be done for me: leave me alone two months, that I may go up and down on the mountains and weep because of my virginity, I and my companions." <sup>38</sup> And he said, "Go." So he sent her away for two months; and **she left with her companions, and wept on the mountains because of her virginity**. <sup>39</sup> At the end of two months she returned to her father, who **did to her according to the vow that he had made**; and she never known a man.⁸ Thus it became a custom in Israel, <sup>40</sup> that the daughters of Israel went year by year **to commemorate⁹ the daughter** of Jephthah the Gileadite four days in the year.

It is true; to infer that having the idea of an animal sacrifice would really have not been an impressive vow, which the context requires. Human sacrifice will be repugnant if we are talking about taking a life. Jephthah had no sons, so he likely knew it was the daughter, who would come to greet him.

First, the text does not say he killed his daughter. The idea of some that he did kill her is concluded only by inference. While it is not good policy to interpret backward, using Paul on Judges, he does say humans are to be **"as a living sacrifice."** Therefore, Jephthah could

---

⁸ I.e., *never had relations with a man*
⁹ Or *lament*

have offered his daughter at the temple, "as a living sacrifice" in service, like Samuel.

This is not to be taken dismissively, because, under Jewish backgrounds, it is no small thing to offer a **perpetual virginity** as a sacrifice. This would mean Jephthah's lineage would not be carried on, the family name, was no more.

Second, the context says she went out to weep for two months, not mourn her death. It says, "she left with her companions, and **wept on the mountains because of her virginity.**"

If she was facing imminent death, she could have married, and spent that last two months as a married woman. There would be absolutely no reason for her to mourn her virginity if she were not facing perpetual virginity. – Exodus 38:8; 1 Samuel 2:22

Third, it was completely forbidden to offer a human sacrifice. – Leviticus 18:21; 20:2-5; Deuteronomy 12:31; 18:10

Imagine an Israelite believing that he could please God with a human sacrifice that was intended to offer up a human life. To do so would have been a rejection of Jehovah's Sovereignty (the very person you are asking for help), and a rejection of the Law that made them a special people. Worse still, this interpretation would have us believe that Jehovah knew this was coming, allowed the vow, and then aided this type of man to succeed over his enemies.

The last point is simple enough. If such a man as one who would make such a vow, in gross violation of the law, and then carry it out; there is no way he would be mentioned by Paul in Hebrews chapter 11 among the most faithful men and women in Israelite history.

In review, there is no way God would have granted and helped in Jephthah's initial success knowing the vow that was coming because both Jehovah and Jephthah would be as bad as the Canaanites. There is no way that God would accept such a vow and then go on to help Jephthah with his enemies yet again. Then, to allow such a vow to be carried out, to then put Jephthah on the wall of star witnesses for God in Hebrews chapter 11.

### Does Isaiah 45:7 mean that God Is the Author of Evil?

| Isaiah 45:7 King James Version (KJV) | Isaiah 45:7 English Standard Version (ESV) |
|---|---|
| [7] I form the light, and create darkness: I make peace, and **create evil**: I the Lord do all these things. | [7] I form light and create darkness, I make well-being and **create calamity**, I am the Lord, who does all these things.[10] |

**Encarta Dictionary:** (Evil) (1) morally bad: profoundly immoral or wrong (2) deliberately causing great harm, pain, or upset

**QUESTION:** Is this view of evil always the case? No, as you will see below.

Some apologetic authors try to say, 'we do not understand Isaiah 45:7 correctly, because there are other verses that say God is not evil (1 John 1:5), cannot look approvingly on evil (Hab. 1:13), and cannot be tempted by evil. (James 1:13)' Well, while all of these things are Scripturally true, the question at hand is not: Is God evil, can God approvingly look on evil, or can God be tempted with evil? Those questions are not relevant to the one at hand, as God cannot be those things, and at the same time, he can be the yes to our question. The question is, is God the author, the creator of evil?

---

[10] See Jeremiah 18:11, Lamentations 3:18, and Amos 3:6

We would hardly argue that God was **not just** in his bringing "calamity" or "evil" down on Adam and Eve. Thus, we have Isaiah 45:7 saying that God is the creator of "calamity" or "evil."

Let us begin simple, without trying to be philosophical. When God removed Adam and Eve from the Garden of Eden, he sentenced them and humanity to sickness, old age, and death. (Rom. 5:8; i.e., enforce penalty for sin), which was to bring "calamity" or "evil" upon humankind. Therefore, as we can see "evil" does not always mean wrongdoing. Other examples of God bringing "calamity" or "evil" are Noah and the flood, the Ten Plagues of Egypt, and the destruction of the Canaanites. These acts of evil were not acts of wrongdoing. Rather, they were righteous and just, because God, the Creator of all things, was administering justice to wrongdoers, to sinners. He warned the perfect first couple what the penalty was for sin. He warned the people for a hundred years by Noah's preaching. He warned the Canaanites centuries before.

Nevertheless, there are times, when God extends mercy, refraining from the execution of his righteous judgment to one worthy of calamity. For example, he warned Nineveh, the city of blood, and they repented, so he pardoned them. (Jonah 3:10) God has made it a practice to warn persons of the results of sin, giving them undeservedly many opportunities to change their ways. – Ezekiel 33:11.

God cannot sin; it is impossible for him to do so. So, when did he create evil? Without getting into the eternity of his knowing what he was going to do, and when, let us just say, evil did not exist when he was the only person in existence. We might say the idea of evil existed because he knew what he was going to do. However, the moment he created creatures (spirit and human), the potential for evil came into existence because both have free will to sin (fall short of perfection). Evil became a reality the moment Satan entertained the idea of causing Adam to sin, to get humanity for himself, and then acted on it.

God has the right and is just to bring the *calamity of* or *evil* down on anyone that is an unrepentant sinner. God did not even have to give us the underserved kindness of offering us his Son. God is the author or agent of evil regardless of the source books that claim otherwise. If he had never created free will beings, evil would have never gone from the idea of evil to the potential of evil, to the existence of evil. However, God felt that it was better to get the sinful state out of angel and human existence, recover, and then any who would sin thereafter; he would be justified in handing out evil or calamity to only that person or angel alone.

Who among us would argue that he should have created humans and angels like robots, automatons with no free will? The moment he chose the free will, he moved evil from an idea to a potential, and Satan moved it to reality. God has a moral nature that does not bring about evil and sin when he is the only person in existence. However, the moment he created beings in his image, which had the potential to sin, he brought about evil. The moment we have a moral code of good and evil that is placed upon one's with free will; then, we have evil as a potential.

In English, the very comprehensive Hebrew word ra' is variously translated as "bad," "downcast (sad, NASB)," "ugly," "evil," "grievous (distressing, NASB)," "sore," "selfish (stingy, HCSB)," and "envious," depending upon the context. (Gen 2:9; 40:7; 41:3; Ex 33:4; Deut. 6:22; 28:35; Pro 23:6; 28:22)

Evil as an adjective describes the quality of a class of people, places, or things, or of a specific person, place, or thing

**Evil** as a noun, **defines** the **nature** of a class of people, places, or things, or of a specific person, place, or thing (e.g., the evil one, evil eye).

We can agree that "evil" is a thing. Create means to bring something into existence, be it people, places, or things, as well something abstract, for lack of a better word at the moment. We would agree that when God was alone evil was not a reality; it did not exist? We would agree that the moment that God created free will creatures (angels and humans), creating humans in his image, with his moral nature, he also brought the potential for evil into existence, and it was realized by Satan?

## Inerrancy: Can the Bible Be trusted?

If the Bible is the Word of God, it should be in complete agreement throughout; there should be no contradictions. Yet, the rational mind must ask, why is it that some passages appear to be contradictions when compared with others? For example, Numbers 25:9 tells us that 24,000 died from the scourge, whereas at 1 Corinthians 10:8, the apostle Paul says it was 23,000. This would seem to be a clear error. Before addressing such matters, let us first look at some background information.

*Full inerrancy* in this book means that the original writings are fully without error in all that they state, as are the words. The words were not dictated (automaton), but the intended meaning is inspired, as are the words that convey that meaning. The Author allowed the writer to use his style of writing, yet controlled the meaning to the extent of not allowing the writer to choose a wrong word, which would not convey the intended meaning. Other more liberal-minded persons hold with *partial inerrancy*, which claims that as far as faith is concerned, this portion of God's Word is without error, but that there are historical, geographical, and scientific errors.

There are several different levels of inerrancy. *Absolute Inerrancy* is the belief that the Bible is fully true and exact in every way; including not only relationships and doctrine, but also science and history. In other words, all information is completely exact. *Full Inerrancy* is the belief that the Bible was not written as a science or historical textbook, but is phenomenological, in that it is written from the human perspective. In other words, speaking of such things as the sun rising, the four corners of the earth or the rounding off of number approximations are all from a human perspective. *Limited Inerrancy* is the belief that the Bible is meant only as a reflection of God's purposes and will, so the science and history is the understanding of the author's day, and is limited. Thus, the Bible is susceptible to errors in these areas. *Inerrancy of Purpose* is the belief that it is only inerrant in the purpose of bringing its readers to a saving faith. The Bible is not about facts, but about persons and relationships, thus, it is subject to error. *Inspired: Not Inerrant* is the belief that its authors are human and thus subject to human error. It should be noted that this author holds the position of full inerrancy.

For many today, the Bible is nothing more than a book written by men. The Bible critic believes the Bible to be full of myths and legends, contradictions, and geographical, historical, and scientific errors. University professor Gerald A. Larue had this to say, "The views of the writers as expressed in the Bible reflect the ideas, beliefs, and concepts current in their own times and are limited by the extent of knowledge in those times."[11] On the other hand, the Bible's authors claim that their writings were inspired of God, as Holy Spirit moved them along. We will discover shortly that the Bible critics have much to say, but it is inflated or empty.

---

[11] Gerald Larue, "The Bible as a Political Weapon," *Free Inquiry* (Summer 1983): 39.

**2 Timothy 3:16-17** Updated American Standard Version (UASV)

[16] All Scripture is inspired by God and profitable for teaching, for reproof, for correction, for training in righteousness; [17] so that the man of God may be fully competent, equipped for every good work.

**2 Peter 1:21** Updated American Standard Version (UASV)

[21] for no prophecy was ever produced by the will of man, but men carried along by the Holy Spirit spoke from God.

The question remains as to whether the Bible is a book written by imperfect men and full of errors, or is written by imperfect men, but inspired by God. If the Bible is just another book by imperfect man, there is no hope for humankind. If it is inspired by God and without error, although penned by imperfect men, we have the hope of everything that it offers: a rich, happy life now by applying counsel that lies within and the real life that is to come, everlasting life. This author contends that the Bible is inspired of God and free of human error, although written by imperfect humans.

Before we take on the critics who seem to sift the Scriptures looking for problematic verses, let us take a moment to reflect on how we should approach these alleged problem texts. The critic's argument goes something like this: 'If God does not err and the Bible is the Word of God, then the Bible should not have one single error or contradiction, yet it is full of errors and contradictions.' If the Bible is riddled with nothing but contradictions and errors as the critics would have us believe, why, out of 31,173 verses in the Bible, should there be only 2-3 thousand Bible difficulties that are called into question, this being less than ten percent of the whole?

First, let it be said that it is every Christian's obligation to get a deeper understanding of God's Word, just as the apostle Paul told Timothy:

**1 Timothy 4:15-16** Updated American Standard Version (UASV)

[15] Practice these things, be absorbed in them, so that your progress will be evident to all. [16] Pay close attention to yourself and to your teaching; persevere in these things, for as you do this you will ensure salvation both for yourself and for those who hear you.

Paul also told the Corinthians:

**2 Corinthians 10:4-5** Updated American Standard Version (UASV)

[4] For the weapons of our warfare are not of the flesh[12] but powerful to God for destroying strongholds.[13] [5] We are destroying speculations and every lofty thing raised up against the knowledge of God, and we are taking every thought captive to the obedience of Christ,

Paul also told the Philippians:

**Philippians 1:7** Updated American Standard Version (UASV)

[7] It is right for me to feel thus about you all, because I hold you in my heart, for you are all partakers with me of grace, both in my imprisonment and in the defense and confirmation of the gospel.

In being able to defend against the modern-day critic, one has to be able to reason from the Scriptures and overturn the critic's argument(s) with mildness. If someone were to approach us about an alleged error or contradiction, what should we do? We should be frank and honest. If we do not have an answer, we should admit

---

[12] That is *merely human*
[13] That is *tearing down false arguments*

such. If the text in question gives the appearance of difficulty, we should admit this as well. If we are unsure as to how we should answer, we can simply say that we will look into it and get back to them, returning with a reasonable answer.

However, we do not want to express disbelief and doubt to our critics, because they will be emboldened in their disbelief. It will put them on the offense and us on the defense. With great confidence, we can express that there is an answer. The Bible has withstood the test of 2,000 years of persecution and interrogation and yet it is the most printed book of all time, currently being translated into 2,287 languages. If these critical questions were so threatening, the Bible would not be the book that it is.

When we are pursuing the text in question, be unwavering in purpose, or resolved to find an answer. In some cases, it may take hours of digging to find the solution. Consider this: as we resolve these difficulties, we are also building our faith that God's Word is inerrant. Moreover, we will want to do preventative maintenance in our personal study. As we are doing our Bible reading, take note of these surface discrepancies and resolve them as we work our way through the Bible. We need to make this part of our prayers as well. I recommend the following program. Below are several books that deal with difficult passages. As we daily read and study our Bible from Genesis to Revelation, do not attempt it in one year; make it a four-year program. Use a good exegetical commentary like *The Holman Old/New Testament Commentary* (HOTC/HNTC) or *The New American Commentary* set, and *The Big Book of Bible Difficulties* by Norman L. Geisler, as well as *The Encyclopedia of Bible Difficulties* by Gleason Archer.

We should be aware that men under inspiration penned the originally written books. In fact, we do not have those originals, what textual scholars call autographs, but we do have thousands of copies. The copyists, however, were not inspired; therefore, as one might expect, throughout the first 1,400 years of copying, thousands of errors were transmitted into the texts that were being copied by imperfect hands that were not under inspiration when copying. Yet, the next 450 years saw a restoration of the text by textual scholars from around the world. Therefore, while many of our best literal translations today may not be inspired, they are a mirror-like reflection of the autographs by way of textual criticism.[14] Therefore, the fallacy could be with the copyist error that has simply not been weeded out. In addition, we must keep in mind that God's Word is without error, but our interpretation and understanding of that Word is not.

It should be noted that the Bible is made up of 66 smaller books that were hand-written over a period of 1,600 years, having some 40 writers of various trades such as shepherd, king, priest, tax collector, governor, physician, copyist, fisherman, and a tentmaker. Therefore, it should not surprise us that some difficulties are encountered as we casually read the Bible. Yet, if one were to take a deeper look, one would find that these difficulties are easily explained. Let us take a few pages to examine some passages that have been under attack.

This chapter's objective is not to be exhaustive, not even close. What we are looking to do is cover a few alleged contradictions and a couple of alleged mistakes. This is to give us a small sampling of the reasonable answers that we will find in the above recommended books. Remember, our Bible is a sword that we must use both offensively and defensively. One must wonder how

---

[14] Textual criticism is the study of copies of any written work of which the autograph (original) is unknown, with the purpose of ascertaining the original text. Harold J. Green, Introduction to New Testament Textual Criticism (Peabody, MA: Hendrickson, 1995), 1.

long a warrior of ancient times would last who was not expertly trained in the use of his weapon. Let us look at a few scriptures that support our need to learn our Bible well so will be able to defend what we believe to be true.

When "false apostles, deceitful workmen, disguising themselves as apostles of Christ" were causing trouble in the congregation in Corinth, the apostle Paul wrote that under such circumstances, we are to *tear down their arguments* and *take every thought captive.* (2 Corinthians 10:4, 5; 11:13–15) All who present critical arguments against God's Word, or contrary to it, can have their arguments overturned by the Christian, who is able and ready to defend that Word in mildness. – 2 Timothy 2:24–26.

**1 Peter 3:15** Updated American Standard Version (UASV)

[15] but sanctify Christ as Lord in your hearts, always being prepared to make a defense[15] to anyone who asks you for a reason for the hope that is in you; yet do it with gentleness and respect;

Peter says that we need to be prepared to make a *defense.* The Greek word behind the English 'defense' is *apologia,* which is actually a legal term that refers to the defense of a defendant in court. Our English apologetics is just what Peter spoke of, having the ability to give a reason to any who may challenge us, or to answer those who are not challenging us but who have honest questions that deserve to be answered.

**2 Timothy 2:24-25** Updated American Standard Version (UASV)

[24] For a slave of the Lord does not need to fight, but needs to be kind to all, qualified to teach, showing restraint when wronged [25] with gentleness correcting those

---

[15] Or *argument,* or *explanation*

who are in opposition, if perhaps God may grant them repentance leading to accurate knowledge[16] of the truth,

Look at the Greek word (*epignosis*) behind the English "knowledge" in the above. "It is more intensive than *gnosis* (1108), knowledge because it expresses a more thorough participation in the acquiring of knowledge on the part of the learner."[17] The requirement of all of the Lord's servants is that they be able to teach, but not in a quarrelsome way, and in a way to correct his opponents with mildness. Why? Because the purpose of it all is that by God, and through the Christian teacher, one may come to repentance and begin taking in an accurate knowledge of the truth.

## Inerrancy: Practical Principles to Overcoming Bible Difficulties

Below are several ways of looking at the Bible that enable the reader to see he is not dealing with an error or contradiction, but rather a Bible difficulty.

### Different Points of View

At times, you may have two different writers who are writing from two different points of view.

**Numbers 35:14** Updated American Standard Version (UASV)

[14] You shall give three cities across the Jordan and three cities you shall give in the land of Canaan; they will be cities of refuge.

---

[16] *Epignosis* is a strengthened or intensified form of *gnosis* (*epi*, meaning "additional"), meaning, "true," "real," "full," "complete" or "accurate," depending upon the context. Paul and Peter alone use *epignosis*.

[17] Spiros Zodhiates, *The Complete Word Study Dictionary: New Testament*, Electronic ed. (Chattanooga, TN: AMG Publishers, 2000, c1992, c1993), S. G1922.

**Joshua 22:4** Updated American Standard Version (UASV)

⁴ And now Jehovah your God has given rest to your brothers, as he spoke to them; therefore turn now and go to your tents, to the land of your possession, which Moses the servant of Jehovah gave you beyond the Jordan. [on the other side of the Jordan, ESV]

Here we see that Moses is speaking about the east side of the Jordan when he says "on this side of the Jordan." Joshua, on the other hand, is also speaking about the east side of the Jordan when he says "on the other side of the Jordan." So, who is correct? Both are. When Moses was penning Numbers the Israelites had not yet crossed the Jordan River, so the east side was "this side," the side he was on. On the other hand, when Joshua penned his book, the Israelites had crossed the Jordan, so the east side was just as he had said, "on the other side of the Jordan." Thus, we should not assume that two different writers are writing from the same perspective.

## A Careful Reading

At times, it may simply be a case of needing to slow down and carefully read the account, considering exactly what is being said.

**Joshua 18:28** Updated American Standard Version (UASV)

²⁸ and Zelah, Haeleph and the Jebusite (that is, Jerusalem), Gibeah, Kiriath; fourteen cities with their villages. This is the inheritance of the sons of Benjamin according to their families.

**Judges 1:21** Updated American Standard Version (UASV)

²¹ But the sons of Benjamin did not drive out the Jebusites who lived in Jerusalem; so the Jebusites have lived with the sons of Benjamin in Jerusalem to this day.

**Joshua 15:63** Updated American Standard Version (UASV)

⁶³ But as for the Jebusites, the inhabitants of Jerusalem, the sons of Judah could not drive them out; so the Jebusites live with the sons of Judah at Jerusalem until this day.

**Judges 1:8-9** Updated American Standard Version (UASV)

⁸ And then the sons of Judah fought against Jerusalem and captured it and struck it with the edge of the sword and set the city on fire. ⁹ And afterward the sons of Judah went down to fight against the Canaanites living in the hill country and in the Negev[18] and in the Shephelah.[19]

**2 Samuel 5:5-9** Updated American Standard Version (UASV)

⁵ At Hebron he reigned over Judah seven years and six months, and in Jerusalem he reigned thirty-three years over all Israel and Judah.

⁶ And the king and his men went to Jerusalem against the Jebusites, the inhabitants of the land, and they said to David, "You shall not come in here, but the blind and lame will turn you away"; thinking, "David cannot come in here." ⁷ Nevertheless, David captured the stronghold of Zion, that is the city of David. ⁸ And David said on that day, "Whoever would strike the Jebusites, let him get up the water shaft to attack 'the lame and the blind,' who are hated by David's soul." Therefore it is said, "The blind and the lame shall not come into the house." ⁹ And David lived

[18] I.e. *South*
[19] I.e., lowland

in the stronghold and called it the city of David. And David built all around from the Millo and inward.

There is no doubt that even the advanced Bible reader of many years can come away confused because the above accounts seem to be contradictory. In Joshua 18:28 and Judges 1:21, we see that Jerusalem was an inheritance of the tribe of Benjamin, yet the Benjamites were unable to conquer Jerusalem. However, in Joshua 15:63 we see that the tribe of Judah could not conquer them either, with the reading giving the impression that it was a part of their inheritance. In Judges 1:8, however, Judah was eventually able to conquer Jerusalem and burn it with fire. Yet, to add even more to the confusion, we find at 2 Samuel 5:5–8 that David is said to have conquered Jerusalem hundreds of years later.

Now that we have the particulars let us look at it more clearly. The boundary between Benjamin's inheritances ran right through the middle of Jerusalem. Joshua 8:28 is correct, in that what would later be called the "city of David" was in the territory of Benjamin, but it also in part crossed over the line into the territory of Judah, causing both tribes to go to war against this Jebusite city. It is also true that the tribe of Benjamin was unable to conquer the city and that the tribe of Judah eventually did. However, if you look at Judges 1:9 again, you will see that Judah did not finish the job entirely and moved on to conquer other areas. This allowed the remaining ones to regroup and form a resistance that neither Benjamin nor Judah could overcome, so these Jebusites remained until the time of David, hundreds of years later.

## Intended Meaning of Writer

First, the Bible student needs to understand the level that the Bible intends to be exact in what is written. If Jim told a friend that 650 graduated with him from high school in 1984, it is not challenged, because it is all too clear that he is using rounded numbers and is not meaning to be exactly precise. This is how God's Word operates as well. Sometimes it means to be exact, at other times, it is simply rounding numbers, in other cases, the intention of the writer is a general reference, to give readers of that time and succeeding generations some perspective. Did Samuel, the author of judges, intend to pen a book on the chronology of Judges, or was his focus on the falling away, oppression, and the rescue by a judge, repeatedly. Now, it would seem that Jeremiah, the author of 1 Kings was more interested in giving his readers an exact number of years.

**Acts 2:41** Updated American Standard Version (UASV)

[41] So those who received his word were baptized, and there were added that day about three thousand souls.

As you can see here, numbers within the Bible are often used with approximations. This is a frequent practice even today, in both written works and verbal conversation.

**Acts 7:2-3** Updated American Standard Version (UASV)

[2] And Stephen said:

"Brothers and fathers, hear me. The God of glory appeared to our father Abraham when he was in Mesopotamia, before he lived in Haran, [3] and said to him, 'Go out from your land and from your kindred and go into the land that I will show you.'

If you were to check the Hebrew Scriptures at Genesis 12:1, you would find that what is claimed to have been said by God to Abraham is not quoted word-for-word; it is simply a paraphrase. This is a normal practice within Scripture and in writing in general.

**Numbers 34:15** Updated American Standard Version (UASV)

¹⁵ The two and a half tribes have received their inheritance beyond the Jordan opposite Jericho, eastward toward the sunrising."

Just as you would read in today's local newspaper, the Bible writer has written from the human standpoint, how it appeared to him. The Bible also speaks of "to the end of the earth" (Psalm 46:9), "from the four corners of the earth" (Isa 11:12), and "the four winds of the earth" (Revelation 7:1). These phrases are still used today.

## Unexplained Does Not mean Unexplainable

Considering that there are 31,173 verses in the Bible, encompassing 66 books written by about 40 writers, ranging from shepherds to kings, an army general, fishermen, tax collector, a physician and on and on, and being penned over a 1,600 year period, one does find a few hundred Bible difficulties (about one percent). However, 99 percent of those are explainable. Yet no one wants to be so arrogant to say that he can explain them all. It has nothing to do with the inadequacy of God's Word but is based on human understanding. In many cases, science or archaeology and the field of custom and culture of ancient peoples has helped explain difficulties in hundreds of passages. Therefore, there may be less than one percent left to be answered, yet our knowledge of God's Word continues to grow.

## Unrealistic Expectations Are Unhelpful Expectations

We should also note that **Unrealistic expectations** are unhelpful **expectations**. Even though it's challenging to set aside what we expect, hope, or desire a particular Bible book to tell us, work on relinquishing them unrealistic expectations because they can actually lead to doubt. And remember that God's Word of 39 OT books and 27 NT books, a total of 66 books are giving us exactly what we need to get through life or up unto the time of Christ's second coming. That understanding alone should actually inspire, support, and serve us well.

Remember (1) the intent of the Bible author is not meant to fulfill our expectations of what we want; the intention is to give the reader God's will and purposes. (2) A Bible book cannot be what it was not meant to be. An illustration of a book that is on the subject we might want, say a cookbook on cookies, yet after buying it, we find that it does not have the recipe for our favorite cookies. Yet, this does not mean the cookbook is worthless. A book on THE TEXT OF THE NEW TESTAMENT may come in the mail, and we might have been expecting an introductory level book. However, it ended up with an intermediate-advanced book, so do we go to Amazon and give a 1-star review, complaining about how the book was not what we wanted? Is that the author's fault that the customer had an unrealistic expectation, especially when the book description and the look-Inside-Feature made it clear what the intent of the author was?

## Guilty Until Proven Innocent

This is exactly the perception that the critic has of God's Word. The legal principle of being "innocent until proven guilty" afforded mankind in courts of justice is withheld from the very Word of God. What is ironic here is that this policy has contributed to these Bible critics looking foolish over and over again when something comes to light that vindicates the portion of Scripture they are challenging.

**Daniel 5:1** Updated American Standard Version (UASV)

[1] Belshazzar the king made[20] a great feast for a thousand of his nobles, and he was drinking wine in the presence of the thousand.

Bible critics had long claimed that Belshazzar was not known outside of the book Daniel; therefore, they argue that Daniel was mistaken. Yet it hardly seems prudent to argue error from absence of outside evidence. Just because archaeology had not discovered such a person did not mean that Daniel was wrong, or that such a person did not exist. In 1854, some small clay cylinders were discovered in modern-day southern Iraq, which would have been the city of Ur in ancient Babylonia. The cuneiform documents were a prayer of King Nabonidus for "Bel-sar-ussur, my eldest son." These tablets also showed that this "Bel-sar-ussur" had secretaries as well as a household staff. Other tablets were discovered a short time later that showed that the kingship was entrusted to this eldest son as a coregent while his father was away.

He entrusted the 'Camp' to his oldest (son), the firstborn [Belshazzar], the troops everywhere in the country he ordered under his (command). He let (everything) go, entrusted the kingship to him and, himself, he [Nabonidus] started out for a long journey, the (military) forces of Akkad marching with him; he turned towards Tema (deep) in the west."[21]

## Ignoring Literary Styles

The Bible is a diverse book when it comes to literary styles: narrative, poetic, prophetic, and apocalyptic; also containing parables, metaphors, similes, hyperbole, and

---

[20] I.e., held
[21] J. Pritchard, ed., *Ancient Near Eastern Texts* (1974), 313.

other figures of speech. Too often, these alleged errors are the result of a reader taking a figure of speech as literal, or reading a parable as though it is a narrative.

**Matthew 24:35** Updated American Standard Version (UASV)

[35] Heaven and earth will pass away, but my words will not pass away.

If some do not recognize that they are dealing with a figure of speech, they are bound to come away with the wrong meaning. Some have concluded from Matthew 24:35 that Jesus was speaking of an eventual destruction of the earth. This is hardly the case, as his listeners would not have understood it that way based on their understanding of the Old Testament. They would have understood that he was simply being emphatic about the words he spoke, using hyperbole. What he was conveying is that his words are more enduring than heaven and earth, and with heaven and earth being understood as eternal, this merely conveyed even more so that Jesus' words could be trusted.

## Two Accounts of the Same Incident

If you were to speak to officers that take accident reports for their police department, you would find that there is cohesion in the accounts, but each person has merely witnessed aspects that have stood out to them. We will see that this is the case as well with the examples below, which is the same account in two different gospels:

**Matthew 8:5** Updated American Standard Version (UASV)

[5] When he[22] had entered Capernaum, a centurion came forward to him, imploring him,

---

[22] That is *Jesus*

**Luke 7:2-3** Updated American Standard Version (UASV)

2 And a centurion's[23] slave, who was highly regarded[24] by him, was sick and about to die. 3 When he heard about Jesus, he sent some older men of the Jews[25] asking him to come and bring his slave safely through.[26]

Immediately we see the problem of whether the centurion or the elders of the Jews spoke with Jesus. The solution is not really hidden from us. Which of the two accounts is the most detailed account? You are correct if you said, Luke. The centurion sent the elders of the Jews to represent him to Jesus, so; that whatever response Jesus might give, it would be as though he were addressing the centurion; therefore, Matthew gave his readers the basic thought, not seeing the need of mentioning the elders of the Jews aspect. This is how a representative was viewed in the first century, just as some countries see ambassadors today as being the very person they represent. Therefore, both Matthew and Luke are correct.

## Man's Fallible Interpretations

Inspiration by God is infallible, without error. Imperfect man and his interpretations over the centuries, as bad as many of them have been, should not cast a shadow over God's inspired Word. The entire Word of God has one meaning and one meaning only for every penned word, which is what God willed to be conveyed by the human writer he chose to use.

### The Autograph Alone Is Inspired and Inerrant

---

23 I.e., army officer over a hundred solderiers
24 Lit *to whom he was honorable*
25 Or *Jewish elders*
26 I.e., *save the life of his slave*

EDWARD D. ANDREWS

It has been argued by conservative scholars that only the autograph manuscripts were inspired and inerrant, not the copying of those manuscripts over the next 3,000 years for the Old Testament and 1,500 years for the New Testament. While I would agree with this position as well, it should be noted that we do not possess the autographs, so to argue that they are inerrant is to speak of nonexistent documents. However, it should be further understood that through the science of textual criticism, we can establish a mirror reflection of the autograph manuscripts. B. F. Westcott, F. J. A. Hort, F. F. Bruce, and many other textual scholars would agree with Norman L Geisler's assessment: "The New Testament, then, has not only survived in more manuscripts than any other book from antiquity, but it has survived in a purer form than any other great book—*a form that is 99.5 percent pure.*"[27]

An example of a copyist error can be found in Luke's genealogy of Jesus at Luke 3:35–37. In verse 37 you will find a Cainan, and in verse 36 you will find a second Cainan between Arphaxad (Arpachshad) and Shelah. As one can see from most footnotes in different study Bibles, the Cainan in verse 36 is seen as a scribal error, and is not found in the Hebrew Old Testament, the Samaritan Pentateuch, or the Aramaic Targums, but is found in the Greek Septuagint. (Genesis 10:24; 11:12, 13; 1 Chronicles 1:18, but not 1 Chronicles 1:24) It seems quite unlikely that it was in the earlier copies of the Septuagint, because the first-century Jewish historian Josephus lists Shelah next as the son of Arphaxad, and Josephus normally followed the Septuagint.[28] So one might ask why this second Cainan is found in the translations at all if this is the case? The manuscripts that do contain this second Cainan are some of the best manuscripts that are used in establishing the

---

[27] Norman L. Geisler and William E. Nix: *A General Introduction to the Bible* (Chicago, Moody Press, 1980), 367. (Emphasis is mine.)
[28] *Jewish Antiquities*, I, 146 [vi, 4].

original text: 01 B L A¹ 33 (Kainam); A 038 044 0102 A¹³ (Kainan).

### Look at the Context

Many alleged inconsistencies disappear by simply looking at the context. Taking words out of context can distort their meaning. *Merriam-Webster's Collegiate Dictionary* defines context as "the parts of a discourse that surround a word or passage and can throw light on its meaning."[29] Context can also be "the circumstances or events that form the environment within which something exists or takes place." If we were to look in a thesaurus for a synonym, we would find "background" for this second meaning. At 2 Timothy 2:15, the apostle Paul brings home the point of why context is so important: "Do your best to present yourself to God as one approved, a worker who has no need to be ashamed, rightly handling the word of truth."

**Ephesians 2:8-9** Updated American Standard Version (UASV)

⁸ For by grace you have been saved through faith; and that not of yourselves, it is the gift of God; ⁹ not from works, so that no man may boast.

**James 2:26** Updated American Standard Version (UASV)

²⁶ For as the body apart from the spirit[30] is dead, so also faith apart from works is dead.

So, which is it? Is salvation possible by faith alone as Paul wrote to the Ephesians, or is faith dead without works as James wrote to his readers? As our subtitle brings out, let us look at the context. In the letter to the Ephesians, the apostle Paul is speaking to the Jewish Christians who were

---

[29] Merriam-Webster, Inc: *Merriam-Webster's Collegiate Dictionary*. Eleventh ed. (Springfield, Mass.: Merriam-Webster, Inc. 2003).
[30] Or *breath*

looking to the works of the Mosaic Law as a means to salvation, a righteous standing before God. Paul was telling these legalistic Jewish Christians that this is not so. In fact, this would invalidate Christ's ransom because there would have been no need for it if one could achieve salvation by meticulously keeping the Mosaic Law. (Rom. 5:18) But James was writing to those in a congregation who were concerned with their status before other men, who were looking for prominent positions within the congregation, and not taking care of those that were in need. (Jam. 2:14–17) So, James is merely addressing those who call themselves Christian, but in name only. No person could truly be a Christian and not possess some good works, such as feeding the poor, helping the elderly. This type of work was an evident demonstration of one's Christian personality. Paul was in perfect harmony with James on this. – Romans 10:10; 1 Corinthians 15:58; Ephesians 5:15, 21–33; 6:15; 1 Timothy 4:16; 2 Timothy 4:5; Hebrews 10:23-25.

## Inerrancy: Are There Contradictions?

Below I will follow this pattern. I will list the critic's argument first, followed by the text of difficulty, and conclude with an answer to the critic. What should be kept at the forefront of our mind is this: one is simply looking for the best answer, not absoluteness. If there is a reasonable answer to a Bible difficulty, why are the critics able to set them aside with ease? Because they start with the premise that this is not the Word of God, but only a book by imperfect men and full of contradictions; thus, the bias toward errors has blinded their judgment.

**Critic:** The critic would argue that there was an Adam and Eve, and an Abel who was now dead, so, where did Cain get his wife? This is one of the most common questions by Bible critics.

**Genesis 4:17** Updated American Standard Version (UASV)

[17] Cain had sexual relations[31] with his wife and she conceived, and gave birth to Enoch; and he built a city, and called the name of the city Enoch, after the name of his son, Enoch.

**Answer:** If one were to read a little further along, they would come to the realization that Adam had a son named Seth; it further adds that Adam "became father to sons *and daughters.*" (Genesis 5:4) Adam lived for a total of 800 years after fathering Seth, giving him ample opportunity to father many more sons and daughters. So it could be that Cain married one of his sisters. If he waited until one of his brothers and sisters had a daughter, he could have married one of his nieces once she was old enough. In the beginning, humans were closer to perfection; this explains why they lived longer and why at that time there was little health risk of genetic defects in the case of children born to closely related parents, in contrast to how it is today. As time passed, genetic defects increased, and life spans decreased. Adam lived to see 930 years. Yet Shem, who lived after the Flood, died at 600 years, while Shem's son Arpachshad only lived 438 years, dying before his father died. Abraham saw an even greater decrease in that he only lived 175 years while his grandson Jacob was 147 years when he died. Thus, due to increasing imperfection, God prohibited the marriage of closely related people under the Mosaic Law because of the likelihood of genetic defects. – Leviticus 18:9.

**Critic:** If God is here hardening Pharaoh's heart, what exactly makes Pharaoh responsible for the decisions he makes?

---

[31] Lit *knew*

**Exodus 4:21** Updated American Standard Version (UASV)

²¹ Jehovah said to Moses, "When you go and return to Egypt see that you perform before Pharaoh all the wonders which I have put in your hand; but I will harden his heart so that he will not let the people go.

**Answer:** This is actually a prophecy. God knew that what he was about to do would contribute to a stubborn and obstinate Pharaoh, who was going to be unwilling to change or give up the Israelites so they could go off to worship their God. Therefore, this is not stating what God is going to do; it is prophesying that Pharaoh's heart will harden because of the actions of God. The fact is, Pharaoh allowed his own heart to harden because he was determined not to agree with Moses' wishes or accept Jehovah's request to let the people go. Moses tells us at Exodus 7:13 (ESV) that "Pharaoh's heart was hardened, and he would not listen to them, as the Lord had said." Again, at 8:15 we read, "When Pharaoh saw that there was a respite, he hardened his heart and would not listen to them, as the Lord had said."

**Critic:** The Israelites had just received the Ten Commandments, with one commandment being: "You shall not make for yourself a carved image or any likeness of anything that is in heaven above, or that is in the earth beneath, or that is in the water under the earth." Therefore, how is the bronze serpent not a violation of this commandment?

**Numbers 21:9** Updated American Standard Version (UASV)

⁹ And Moses made a bronze serpent and set it on the standard;³² and it came about, that if a serpent bit any man, when he looked to the bronze serpent, he lived.

---

³² I.e., *pole*

THE EPISTLE TO THE HEBREWS

**Answer:** First, an idol is "a representation or symbol of an object of worship; *broadly:* a false god."[33] Second, it should be noted that not all images are idols. The bronze serpent was not made for the purpose of worship, or for some passionate devotion or veneration. There were times, however, when images were created with absolutely no intention of it receiving devotion, veneration, or worship, yet were later made into objects of veneration. That is exactly what happened with the copper serpent that Moses had formed in the wilderness. Many centuries later, "in the third year of Hoshea son of Elah, king of Israel, Hezekiah the son of Ahaz, king of Judah, began to reign. He removed the high places and broke the pillars and cut down the Asherah. And he broke in pieces the bronze serpent that Moses had made; for until those days the people of Israel had made offerings to it (it was called Nehushtan)."—2 Kings 18:1, 4.

**Critic:** Deuteronomy 15:11 (NET) says: "*There will never cease to be some poor people in the land;* therefore, I am commanding you to make sure you open your hand to your fellow Israelites who are needy and poor in your land." Is this not a contradiction of Deuteronomy 15:4? Will there be no poor among the Israelites, or will there be poor among them? Which is it?

**Deuteronomy 15:4** Updated American Standard Version (UASV)

⁴ However, there will be no poor among you, since Jehovah will surely bless you in the land which Jehovah your God is giving you as an inheritance to possess,

**Answer:** If you look at the context, Deuteronomy 15:4 is stating that if the Israelites obey Jehovah's command to take care of the poor, "there should not be any poor among" them. Thus, for every poor person,

---

[33] Merriam-Webster, Inc: *Merriam-Webster's Collegiate Dictionary.* Eleventh ed. (Springfield, Mass.: Merriam-Webster, Inc., 2003).

there will be one to take care of that need. If an Israelite fell on hard times, there was to be a fellow Israelite ready to step in to help him through those hard times. Verse 11 stresses the truth of the imperfect world since the rebellion of Adam and inherited sin: there will always be poor among mankind, the Israelites being no different. However, the difference with God's people is that those who were well off financially were to offset conditions for those who fell on difficult times. This is not to be confused with the socialistic welfare systems in the world today. Those Jews were hard-working men, who labored from sunup to sundown to take care of their families. But if disease overtook their herd or unseasonal weather brought about failed crops, an Israelite could sell himself into the service of a fellow Israelite for a period of time; thereafter, he would be back on his feet. And many years down the road, he may very well do the same for another Israelite, who fell on difficult times.

**Critic:** Joshua 11:23 says that Joshua took the land according to what God had spoken to Moses and handed it on to the nation of Israel as planned. However, in Joshua 13:1, God is telling Joshua that he has grown old and much of the Promised Land has yet to be taken possession of. How can both be true? Is this not a contradiction?

**Joshua 11:23** Updated American Standard Version (UASV)

23 So Joshua took the whole land, according to all that Jehovah had spoken to Moses, and Joshua gave it for an inheritance to Israel according to their divisions by their tribes, and the land had rest from war.

**Joshua 13:1** Updated American Standard Version (UASV)

13 Now Joshua was old and advanced in years, and Jehovah said to him, "You are old and advanced in years, and there remains yet very much land to possess.

**Answer:** No, it is not a contradiction. When the Israelites were to take the land, it was to take place in two different stages: the nation as a whole was to go to war and defeat the 31 kings of this land; thereafter, each Israelite tribe was to take their part of the land based on their individual actions. (Joshua 17:14–18; 18:3) Joshua fulfilled his role, which is expressed in 11:23 while the individual tribes did not complete their campaigns, which is expressed in 13:1. Even though the individual tribes failed to live up to taking their portion, the remaining Canaanites posed no real threat. Joshua 21:44, *ASV,* reads: "Jehovah gave them rest round about."

**Critic:** The critic would point out that John 1:18 clearly says that "*no one has ever seen God,*" while Exodus 24:10 explicitly states that Moses and Aaron, Nadab and Abihu, and seventy of the elders of Israel "*saw the God of Israel.*" Worse still, God informs them in Exodus 33:20: "You cannot see my face, for man shall not see me and live." The critic with his knowing smile says, 'This is a blatant contradiction.'

**John 1:18** Updated American Standard Version (UASV)

[18] No one has seen God at any time; the only begotten god[34] who is in the bosom of the Father,[35] that one has made him fully known.

**Exodus 24:10** Updated American Standard Version (UASV)

[10] and they saw the God of Israel; and under his feet was what seemed like a sapphire pavement, as clear as the sky itself.

---

[34] Jn 1:18: "only-begotten god", P66א*BC*Lsyrhmg.P; **[V1]** "the only-begotten god," P7533אcopbo; **[V2]** "the only-begotten Son." AC3(Wk)QYfl.13 MajVgSyrc

[35] Or *at the Father's side*

EDWARD D. ANDREWS

**Exodus 33:20** Updated American Standard Version (UASV)

20 But he [God] said, "You cannot see my face, for no man can see me and live!"

**Answer:** Exodus 33:20 is one-hundred percent correct: No human could see Jehovah God and live. The apostle Paul at Colossians 1:15 tell us that Christ is the image of the invisible God, and the writer informs us at Hebrews 1:3 that Jesus is the "exact representation of His nature." Yet if you were to read the account of Saul of Tarsus (the apostle Paul), you would see that a mere partial manifestation of Christ's glory blinded Saul – Acts 9:1–18.

When the Bible says that Moses and others have seen God, it is not speaking of *literally* seeing him, because first of all He is an invisible spirit person. It is a *manifestation* of his glory, which is an act of showing or demonstrating his presence, making himself perceptible to the human mind. In fact, it is generally an angelic representative that stands in his place and not him personally. Exodus 24:16 informs us that "the glory of the Lord dwelt on Mount Sinai," not the Lord himself personally. When texts such as Exodus 24:10 explicitly state that Moses and Aaron, Nadab and Abihu, and seventy of the elders of Israel "*saw the God of Israel*," it is this "glory of the Lord," an angelic representative. This is shown to be the case at Luke 2:9, which reads: "And *an angel of the Lord* appeared to them, and *the glory of the Lord shone around them* [the shepherds], and they were filled with fear."

Many Bible difficulties are cleared up elsewhere in Scripture; for example, in the New Testament, you will find a text clarifying a difficulty from the Old Testament, such as Acts 7:53, which refers to those "who received the law *as delivered by angels* and did not keep it." Support comes from Paul at Galatians 3:19: "Why then the law? It was added because of transgressions until the offspring should come to whom the promise had been made, and it was put in place through angels by an intermediary." The writer of Hebrews chimes in at 2:2 with "For since the message *declared by angels* proved to be reliable, and every transgression or disobedience received a just retribution. . . ." As we travel back to Exodus again, to 19:19 specifically, we find support that it was not God's own voice, which Moses heard; no, it was an angelic representative, for it reads: "Moses was speaking, and God was answering him with a voice." Exodus 33:22–23 also helps us to appreciate that it was the back of these angelic representatives of Jehovah that Moses saw: "While my glory passes by . . . Then I will take away my hand, and you shall see my back, but my face shall not be seen."

Exodus 3:4 states: "God called to him out of the bush, 'Moses, Moses!' And he said, 'Here I am.'" Verse 6 informs us: "I am the God of your father, the God of Abraham, the God of Isaac, and the God of Jacob." Yet, in verse 2 we read: "And the angel of the Lord appeared to him in a flame of fire out of the midst of a bush." Here is another example of using God's Word to clear up what seems to be unclear or difficult to understand at first glance. Thus, while it speaks of the Lord making a direct appearance, it is really an angelic representative. Even today, we hear such comments, as 'the president of the United States is to visit the Middle East later this week.' However, later in the article it is made clear that he is not going personally, but it is one of his high-ranking representatives. Let us close with two examples, starting with,

**Genesis 32:24-30** Updated American Standard Version (UASV)

24 And Jacob was left alone, and a man wrestled with him until daybreak. 25 When he saw that he had not prevailed against him, he touched the socket of his thigh; so the socket of Jacob's thigh was dislocated as he wrestled with him. 26 Then he said, "Let me go, for the dawn is breaking." But he said, "I will not let you go unless you

bless me." ²⁷ And he said to him, "What is your name?" And he said, "Jacob." ²⁸ And he said, "Your name shall no longer be called Jacob, but Israel,³⁶ for you have struggled with God and with men and have prevailed." ²⁹ Then Jacob asked him and said, "Please tell me your name." But he said, "Why is it that you ask my name?" And he blessed him there. ³⁰ So Jacob named the place Peniel,³⁷ for he said, "I have seen God face to face, yet my soul has been preserved."

It is all too obvious here that this man is simply a materialized angel in the form of a man, another angelic representative of Jehovah God. Moreover, the reader of this book should have taken in that the Israelites as a whole saw these angelic representatives and spoke of them as though they were dealing directly with Jehovah God himself.

This proved to be the case in the second example found in the book of Judges where an angelic representative visited Manoah and his wife. Like the above mentioned account, Manoah and his wife treated this angelic representative as if he were Jehovah God himself: "And Manoah said to the angel of the Lord, 'What is your name, so that, when your words come true, we may honor you?' And the angel of the Lord said to him, 'Why do you ask my name, seeing it is wonderful?' Then Manoah knew that he was the angel of the Lord. And Manoah said to his wife, "We shall surely die, *for we have seen God.*" – Judges 13:3–22.

## Inerrancy: Are There Mistakes?

I have addressed the alleged contradictions, so it would seem that our job is done here, right? Not hardly.

---

³⁶ Meaning *he contends with God*
³⁷ Meaning *face of God*

Yes, there are just as many who claim that the Bible is full of mistakes.

**Critic:** Matthew 27:5 states that Judas hanged himself, whereas Acts 1:18 says, "Falling headlong, he burst open in the middle and all his intestines gushed out."

**Matthew 27:5** Updated American Standard Version (UASV)

⁵ And he threw the pieces of silver into the temple and departed; and he went away and hanged himself.

**Acts 1:18** Updated American Standard Version (UASV)

¹⁸ (Now this man acquired a field with the price of his wickedness, and falling headlong, he burst open in the middle and all his intestines gushed out.

**Answer:** Neither Matthew nor Luke made a mistake. What you have is Matthew giving the reader the manner in which Judas committed suicide. On the other hand, Luke is giving the reader of Acts, the result of that suicide. Therefore, instead of a mistake, we have two texts that complement each other, really giving the reader the full picture. Judas came to a tree alongside a cliff that had rocks below. He tied the rope to a branch and the other end around his neck and jumped over the edge of the cliff in an attempt at hanging himself. One of two things could have happened: (1) the limb broke plunging him to the rocks below, or (2) the rope broke with the same result, and he burst open onto the rocks below.

**Critic:** The apostle Paul made a mistake when he quotes how many people died.

**Numbers 25:9** Updated American Standard Version (UASV)

⁹ The ones who died in the plague were twenty-four thousand.

**1 Corinthians 10:8** Updated American Standard Version (UASV)

[8] Neither let us commit sexual immorality, as some of them committed sexual immorality, only to fall, twenty-three thousand of them in one day.

**Answer:** We must keep in mind the above principle that we spoke of, the *Intended Meaning of the Writer*. We live in a far more precise age today, where specificity is highly important. However, we round large numbers off (even estimate) all the time: "there were 237,000 people in Time Square last night." The simplest answer is that the number of people slain was in between 23,000 and 24,000, and both writers rounded the number off. However, there is even another possibility, because the book of Numbers specifically speaks of "all the chiefs of the people" (25:4-5), which could account for the extra 1,000, which is mentioned in Numbers 24,000. Thus, you have the people killing the chiefs of the people and the plague killing the people. Therefore, both books are correct.

**Critic:** After 215 years in Egypt, the descendants of Jacob arrived at the Promised Land. As you recall they sinned against God and were sentenced to forty years in the wilderness. But once they entered the Promised Land, they buried Joseph's bones "at Shechem, in the piece of land that *Jacob bought* from the sons of Hamor the father of Shechem," as stated at Joshua 24:32. Yet, when Stephen had to defend himself before the Jewish religious leaders, he said that Joseph was buried "in the tomb that *Abraham had bought* for a sum of silver from the sons of Hamor." Therefore, at once it appears that we have a mistake on the part of Stephen.

**Acts 7:15-16** Updated American Standard Version (UASV)

[15] And Jacob went down to Egypt and died, he and our fathers. [16] And they were brought back to Shechem and

buried in the tomb that Abraham had bought for a sum of silver from the sons of Hamor in Shechem.

**Genesis 23:17-18** Updated American Standard Version (UASV)

[17] So Ephron's field, which was in Machpelah, which faced Mamre, the field and cave which was in it, and all the trees which were in the field, that were in all its border around, were made over [18] to Abraham for a possession in the presence of the sons of Heth, before all who went in at the gate of his city.

**Genesis 33:19** Updated American Standard Version (UASV)

[19] And he bought the piece of land where he had pitched his tent from the hand of the sons of Hamor, Shechem's father, for one hundred qesitahs.[38]

**Joshua 24:32** Updated American Standard Version (UASV)

[32] As for the bones of Joseph, which the sons of Israel brought up from Egypt, they buried them at Shechem, in the piece of land that Jacob bought from the sons of Hamor the father of Shechem for one hundred qesitahs.[39] It became an inheritance of the sons of Joseph.

**Answer:** If we look back to Genesis 12:6-7, we will find that Abraham's first stop after entering Canaan from Haran was Shechem. It is here that Jehovah told Abraham: "To your offspring I will give this land." At this point Abraham built an altar to Jehovah. It seems reasonable that Abraham would need to purchase this land that had not yet been given to his offspring. While it is true that the Old Testament does not mention this purchase, it is likely that Stephen would be aware of such by way of oral

---

[38] Or *pieces of money*; money of unknown value
[39] Or *pieces of money*; money of unknown value

tradition. As Acts chapter seven demonstrates, Stephen had a wide-ranging knowledge of Old Testament history.

Later, Jacob would have had difficulty laying claim to the tract of land that his grandfather Abraham had purchased, because there would have been a new generation of inhabitants of Shechem. This would have been many years after Abraham moved further south and Isaac moved to Beersheba and including Jacob's twenty years in Paddan-aram (Gen 28:6, 7). The simplest answer is that this land was not in use for about 120 years because of Abraham's extensive travels and Isaac's having moved away, leaving it unused; likely it was put to use by others. So, Jacob simply repurchased what Abraham had bought over a hundred years earlier. This is very similar to the time Isaac had to repurchase the well at Beersheba that Abraham had already purchased earlier. – Genesis 21:27–30; 26:26–32.

Genesis 33:18–20 tells us that 'Jacob bought this land for a hundred pieces of money, from the sons of Hamor.' This same transaction is also mentioned at Joshua 24:32, in reference to transporting Joseph's bones from Egypt, to be buried in Shechem.

We should also address the cave of Machpelah that Abraham had purchased in Hebron from Ephron the Hittite. The word "tomb" is not mentioned until Joshua 24:32, and is in reference to the tract of land in Shechem. Nowhere in the Old Testament does it say that Abraham bought a "tomb." The cave of Machpelah obtained by Abraham would eventually become a family tomb, receiving Sarah's body and, eventually, his own, and those of Isaac, Rebekah, Jacob, and Leah. (Genesis 23:14–19; 25:9; 49:30, 31; 50:13) Gleason L. Archer, Jr., concludes this Bible difficulty, saying:

> The reference to a *mnema* ("tomb") in connection with Shechem must either have been proleptic [to anticipate] for the later use of that

shechemite tract for Joseph's tomb (i.e., 'the tomb that Abraham bought' was intended to imply 'the tomb location that Abraham bought"); or else conceivably the dative relative pronoun *ho* was intended elliptically [omission] for *en to topo ho onesato Abraam* ("in the place that Abraham bought") as describing the location of the *mnema* near the Oak of Moreh right outside Shechem. Normally Greek would have used the relative-locative adverb *hou* to express 'in which' or 'where'; but this would have left o*nesato* ("bought") without an object in its own clause, and so *ho* was much more suitable in this context. (Archer 1982, 379–81)

Another solution could be that Jacob is being viewed as a representative of Abraham, for he is the grandson of Abraham. This was quite appropriate in Biblical times, to attribute the purchase to Abraham as the Patriarchal family head.

**Critic:** 2 Samuel 24:1 says that God moved David to count the Israelites, while 1 Chronicles 21:1 Satan, or a resister did. This would seem to be a clear mistake on the part of one of these authors.

**2 Samuel 24:1** Updated American Standard Version (UASV)

¹ Now again the anger of Jehovah burned against Israel, and it incited David against them to say, "Go, number Israel and Judah."

**1 Chronicles 21:1** Updated American Standard Version (UASV)

¹ Then Satan stood up against Israel and moved David to number Israel.

**Answer:** In this period of David's reign, Jehovah was very displeased with Israel, and therefore he did not prevent Satan from bringing this sin on them. Often in Scripture, it is spoken of as though God did something when he allowed an event to take place. For example, it is said that God 'hardened Pharaoh's heart' (Exodus 4:21), when he actually allowed the Pharaoh's heart to harden.

## Inerrancy: Are There Scientific Errors?

Many truths about God are beyond the scope of science. Science and the Bible are not at odds. In fact, we can thank modern day science as it has helped us to better under the creation of God, from our solar system to the universes, to the human body and mind. What we find is a level of order, precision, design, and sophistication, which points to a Designer, the eyes of many Christians, to an Almighty God, with infinite intelligence and power. The apostle Paul makes this all too clear, when he writes, "For his invisible attributes, namely, his eternal power and divine nature, have been clearly perceived, ever since the creation of the world, in the things that have been made. So they are without excuse." – Romans 1:20.

Back in the seventeenth century, the world-renowned scientist Galileo proved beyond any doubt that the earth was not the center of the universe, nor did the sun orbit the earth. In fact, he proved it to be the other way around (no pun intended), with the earth revolving around the sun. However, he was brought up on charges of heresy by the Catholic Church and ordered to recant his position. Why? From the viewpoint of the Catholic Church, Galileo was contradicting God's Word, the Bible. As it turned out, Galileo and science were correct, and the Church was wrong, for which it issued a formal apology in 1992. However, the point we wish to make here is that in all the controversy, the Bible was never in the wrong. It was a misinterpretation on the part of the Catholic Church and not a fault with the Bible. One will find no place in the Bible that claims the sun orbits the earth. So where would the Church get such an idea? The Church got such an idea from Ptolemy (b. about 85 C.E.), an ancient astronomer, who argued for such an idea.

As it usually turns out, the so-called contradiction between science and God's Word lies at the feet of those who are interpreting Scripture incorrectly. To repeat the sentiments of Galileo when writing to a pupil—Galileo expressed the same sentiments: "Even though Scripture cannot err, its interpreters and expositors can, in various ways. One of these, very serious and very frequent, would be when they always want to stop at the purely literal sense."[40] I believe that today's scholars, in hindsight, would have no problem agreeing.

While the Bible is not a science textbook, it is scientifically accurate when it touches on matters of science.

### The Circle of the Earth Hangs on Nothing

**Isaiah 40:22** Updated American Standard Version (UASV)

[22] It is he who sits above **the circle of the earth,**
   and its inhabitants are like grasshoppers;
who stretches out the heavens like a curtain,
   and spreads them like a tent to dwell in.

More than 2,500 years ago, the prophet Isaiah wrote that the earth is a circle or sphere. First, how would it be possible for Isaiah to know the earth is a circle or sphere, if not from inspiration? Scientific America writes, "As countless photos from space can attest, Earth is round—the "Blue Marble," as astronauts have affectionately dubbed it. Appearances, however, can be deceiving. Planet Earth is not, in fact, perfectly round."[41] Scientifically speaking, the

---

[40] Letter from Galileo to Benedetto Castelli, December 21, 1613.
[41] Charles Q. Choi (April 12, 2007). Scientific America. Strange but True: Earth Is Not Round. Retrieved Monday, August 03, 2015.

sun is not perfectly, absolutely 100 percent round but in everyday speech, this verse is both acceptable and accurate, when we keep in mind it is written from a human perspective, not from a scientific perspective. Moreover, Isaiah was not discussing astronomy; he was simply making an inspired observation that man came to realize once he was in space, looking back at the earth, it is round. See the section about title, "Intended Meaning of Writer."

**Job 26:7** Updated American Standard Version (UASV)

> [7] "He stretches out the north over empty space
> and hangs the earth on nothing.

Here the author describes the earth as hanging upon nothing. Many have never heard of the Greek mathematician and astronomer Eratosthenes. He was born in about 276 B.C.E. and received some of his education in Athens, Greece. In 240 B.C., the "Greek astronomer, geographer, mathematician and librarian Eratosthenes calculates the Earth's circumference. His data was rough, but he wasn't far off."[42] While man very early on used their God given intelligence to arrive at some outstanding conclusion that was actually very accurate, we learn two points here. Eratosthenes was a very astute scientist, while Isaiah, who wrote some 500 years earlier, was no scientist at all. Moreover, Moses, who wrote the book of Job over 1,230 years before Eratosthenes, knew that the earth hung upon nothing.

### How Is the Sun Standing Still Possible?

**Joshua 10:13** Updated American Standard Version (UASV)

> [13] And the sun stood still, and the moon stopped,
> until the nation avenged themselves of their enemies.

---

http://www.scientificamerican.com/article/earth-is-not-round/
[42] Alfred, Randy (June 19, 2008). "June 19, 240 B.C.E: The Earth Is Round, and It's This Big". Wired. Retrieved Monday, August 03, 2015.

Is this not written in the Book of Jashar? The sun stopped in the midst of heaven and did not hurry to set for about a whole day.

The Canaanites had besieged the Gibeonites, a group of people that gained Jehovah God's backing because they had faith in Him. In this battle, Jehovah helped the Israelites continue their attack by causing "the sun [to stand] still, and the moon stopped, until the nation took vengeance on their enemies." (Jos 10:1-14) Those who accept God as the creator of the universe and life can accept that he would know a way of stopping the earth from rotating. However, there are other ways of understanding this account. We must keep in mind that the Bible speaks from an earthly observer point of view, so it need not be that he stopped the rotation. It could have been a refraction of solar and lunar light rays, which would have produced the same effect.

**Psalm 136:6** Updated American Standard Version (UASV)

> ⁶ to him who spread out the earth above the waters,
>     for his lovingkindness is everlasting;

**Hebrews 3:4** Updated American Standard Version (UASV)

⁴ For every house is built by someone, but the builder of all things is God.

**2 Kings 20:8-11** Updated American Standard Version (UASV)

⁸ And Hezekiah said to Isaiah, "What shall be the sign that Jehovah will heal me, and that I shall go up to the house of Jehovah on the third day?" ⁹ And Isaiah said, "This shall be the sign to you from Jehovah, that Jehovah will do the thing that he has spoken: shall the shadow go forward ten steps or go back ten steps?" ¹⁰ And Hezekiah answered, "It is an easy thing for the shadow to decline

ten steps; no, but let the shadow turn backward ten steps."
[11] And Isaiah the prophet cried to Jehovah, and he brought the shadow on the steps back ten steps, by which it had gone down on the steps of Ahaz.

**How is it that the stars fought on behalf of Barak?**

**Judges 5:20** Updated American Standard Version (UASV)

[20] From heaven the stars fought, from their courses they fought against Sisera.

**Judges 4:15** Updated American Standard Version (UASV)

[15] And Jehovah routed Sisera and all his chariots and all his army with the edge of the sword before Barak; and Sisera alighted from his chariot and fled away on foot.

In the Bible, you have Biblical prose, and Biblical poetry.

**Prose: language that is not poetry: (1)** writing or speech in its normal continuous form, without the rhythmic or visual line structure of poetry **(2)** ordinary style of expression: writing or speech that is ordinary or matter-of-fact, without embellishment.

**Poetry: literature in verse: (1)** literary works written in verse, in particular verse writing of high quality, great beauty, emotional sincerity or intensity, or profound insight **(2) beauty or grace:** something that resembles poetry in its beauty, rhythmic grace, or imaginative, elevated, or decorative style.

We have a beautiful example of both of these forms of writing communication in chapters four and five of the book of Judges. Judges, Chapter 4 is a prose account of Deborah and Barak, while Judges Chapter 5 is a poetic account. As we have learned from the above, poetry is less concerned with accuracy than evoking emotions. Poetry has a license to say things like what we find in of 5:20, which is in the poetry chapter: "from heaven the stars fought." This can be said, and the reader is expected not to take the language literally. What we can surmise from it though, is that God was acting against Sisera in some way, there was divine intervention.

# Procedures for Handling Biblical Difficulties

1. You need to be completely convinced a reason or understanding exists.

2. You need to have total trust and conviction in the inerrancy of the Scripture as originally written down.

3. You need to study the context and framework of the verse carefully, to establish what the author meant by the words he used. In other words, find the beginning and the end of the context that your passage falls within.

4. You need to understand exegesis: find the historical setting, determine author intent, study key words, and note parallel passages. You need to slow down and carefully read the account, considering exactly what is being said

5. You need to find a reasonable harmonization of parallel passages.

6. You need to consider a variety of trusted Bible commentaries, dictionaries, lexical sources, encyclopedias, as well as books on Bible difficulties.

7. You should investigate as to whether the difficulty is a transmission error in the original text.

8. You must always keep in mind that the historical accuracy of the biblical text is unmatched; that thousands of extant manuscripts some of which date back to the second century B.C. support the transmitted text of Scripture.

9. We must keep in mind that the Bible is a diverse book when it comes to literary styles: narrative, poetic, prophetic, and apocalyptic; also containing parables, metaphors, similes, hyperbole, and other figures of speech. Too often, these alleged errors are the result of a reader taking a figure of speech as literal or reading a parable as though it is a narrative.

10. The Bible student needs to understand what level that the Bible intends to be exact in what is written. If Jim told a friend that 650 graduated with him from high school in 1984, it is not challenged, because it is all too clear that he is using rounded numbers and is not meaning to be precise.

# APPENDIX II Daniel Misjudged

You have a critical body that has formulated an opinion of the Bible, especially prophetic books, long before they have ever looked into the evidence. The liberal critical scholar is anti-supernatural in their mindset. In other words, any book that would claim to have predicted events hundreds of years in advance are simply misrepresenting itself, as that foreknowledge is impossible. Therefore, the book must have been written after the events, yet written in such a way, as to mislead the reader that it was written hundreds of years before.

This is exactly what these critics say we have in the book of Daniel. However, what do we know about the person and the book itself? Daniel is known historically as a man of uprightness in the extreme. The book that he penned has been regarded highly for thousands of years. The context within says that it is authentic and true history, penned by Daniel, a Jewish prophet, who lived in the seventh and sixth centuries B.C.E. The chronology within the book shows that it covers the time period of 616 to 536 B.C.E., being completed by the latter date.

*The New Encyclopædia Britannica* acknowledges that the book of Daniel was once "generally considered to be true history, containing genuine prophecy." However, the *Britannica* asserts that in truth, Daniel "was written in a later time of national crisis—when the Jews were suffering severe persecution under [Syrian King] Antiochus IV Epiphanes." This encyclopedia dates the book between 167 and 164 B.C.E. *Britannica* goes on to assert that the writer of the book of Daniel does not prophesy the future but merely presents "events that are past history to him as prophecies of future happenings."

How does a book and a prophet that has enjoyed centuries of a reputable standing, garner such criticism? It actually began just two-hundred years after Christ, with Porphyry, a philosopher, who felt threatened by the rise of Christianity. His way of dealing with this new religion was to pen fifteen books to undercut it, the twelfth being against Daniel. In the end, Porphyry labeled the book as a forgery, saying that it was written by a second-century B.C.E. Jew. Comparable attacks came in the 18th and 19th centuries. German scholars, who were prejudiced against the supernatural, started modern objections to the Book of Daniel.

As has been stated numerous times in this section, the higher critics and rationalists start with the presupposition that foreknowledge of future events is impossible. As was stated earlier in the chapter on Isaiah, the **important truth for the Bible critic is** the understanding that in all occurrences, prophecy pronounced or written in Bible times meant something to the people of the time it was spoken or written to; it was meant to serve as a guide for them. Frequently, it had specific fulfillment for that time, being fulfilled throughout the lifetime of that very generation. This is actually true; the words always had some application to the very people who heard them. However, the application could be a process of events, starting with the moral condition of the people in their relationship with Jehovah God, which precipitated the prophetic events that were to unfold, even those prophetic events that were centuries away.

However, it must be noted that while Daniel and Isaiah are both prophetic books, Daniel is also known as an apocalyptic book, as is the book of Revelation. This is not to say that Isaiah does not contain some apocalyptic sections (e.g., Isa 24–27; 56–66) What is assumed by the critical scholar here is that there is a rule that a prophet is understood in his day, to be only speaking of the immediate concerns of the people. They are looking at it more like a proclamation, instead of a future event that could be centuries away. Before addressing this concern, let us define apocalyptic for the reader:

## Apocalyptic

This is a term derived from a Greek word meaning "revelation," and used to refer to a pattern of thought and to a form of literature, both dealing with future judgment (eschatology).

Two primary patterns of eschatological thought are found in the Bible, both centered in the conviction that God will act in the near future to save his people and to punish those who oppress them. In prophetic eschatology, the dominant form in the OT, God is expected to act within history to restore man and nature to the perfect condition which existed prior to man's fall. Apocalyptic eschatology, on the other hand, expects God to destroy the old imperfect order before restoring the world to paradise.

## Origins of Apocalypticism

In Israel, apocalyptic eschatology evidently flourished under foreign domination.

From the early 6th century B.C., prophetic eschatology began to decline and apocalyptic eschatology became increasingly popular. The Book of Daniel, written during the 6th century B.C., is the earliest example of apocalyptic literature in existence.[43]

---

[43] Walter A. Elwell and Barry J. Beitzel, *Baker Encyclopedia of the Bible* (Grand Rapids, Mich.: Baker Book House, 1988), 122.

The problem with the modern critic is that he is attempting to look at the Biblical literature through the modern-day mindset. His first error is to believe that a prophetic book was viewed only as a proclamation of current affairs. The Jewish people viewed all prophetic literature just as we would expect, as a book of prophecy. The problem today is that many are not aware of the way they viewed the prophetic literature. While we do not have the space to go into the genre of prophecy and apocalyptic literature extensively, it is recommended that you see Dr. Stein's book in the bibliography at the end of the chapter.

## Some Rules for Prophecy

- One needs to identify the beginning and end of the prophecy.

- The reader needs to find the historical setting.

- The Bible is a diverse book when it comes to literary styles: narrative, poetic, prophetic, and apocalyptic; also containing parables, metaphors, similes, hyperbole, and other figures of speech. Too often, these alleged errors are the result of a reader taking a figure of speech as literal, or reading a parable as though it is a narrative.

- Many alleged inconsistencies disappear by simply looking at the context. Taking words out of context can distort their meaning.

- Determine if the prophet is foretelling the future. On the other hand, is he simply proclaiming God's will and purpose to the people. (If prophetic, has any portion of it been fulfilled?)

- The concept of a second fulfillment should be set aside in place of implications.

- Does the New Testament expound on this prophecy?

- The reader needs to slow down and carefully read the account, considering exactly what is being said.

- The Bible student needs to understand the level that the Bible intends to be exact in what is written. If Jim told a friend that 650 graduated with him from high school in 1984, it is not challenged, because it is all too clear that he is using rounded numbers and is not meaning to be exactly precise.

- Unexplained does not equal unexplainable.

Digging into the ancient Jewish mindset, we find that it is dualistic. It views all of God's creation, either on the side of God or Satan. Further, the Jewish mind was determined that regardless of how bad things were, God would come to the rescue of his people. The only pessimistic thinking was their understanding that there had to be a major catastrophe that precipitated the rescue. In combining this way of thinking, they believed that there are two systems of things: (1) the current wicked one that man lives in, and (2) the one that is to come, where God will restore things to the way it was before Adam and Eve sinned. Jehovah impressed upon his people, to see His rescue as imminent. The vision that comes to Daniel in the book of Daniel and John in the book of Revelations comes in one of two ways: (1) in a dreamed vision state or (2) the person in vision is caught up to heaven and shown what is to take place. Frequently, Isaiah, Daniel, and John did not understand the vision; they were simply to pen what they saw. (Isa 6:9-10; 8:16; 29:9-14; 44:18; 53:1; Dan 8:15–26; 9:20–27; 10:18–12:4; Rev 7:13–17; 17:7–18) The people readily recognized the symbolism in most of the prophetic literature, and the less common symbolisms in apocalyptic literature were far more complex, which by design, heighten the desire to interpret and understand them. There are two very important points to keep in mind: (1) some were not meant to be understood fully at the time, and (2) only the righteous ones would have insight into these books, while the wicked would refuse to understand the spiritual things.

**Daniel 8:26-27** Updated American Standard Version (UASV)

26 The vision of the evenings and the mornings that has been told is true,[44] but seal up the vision,[45] for it refers to many days from now."[46]

27 And I, Daniel, was exhausted and sick for days. Then I got up and carried out the business of the king, and I was disturbed over the vision and no one could understand it.[47]

**Daniel 10:14** Updated American Standard Version (UASV)

14 Now I have come to give you an understanding of what will happen to your people in the end of the days, for it is a vision yet for the days to come."

**Daniel 12:3-4** Updated American Standard Version (UASV)

3 And the ones who are wise will shine brightly like the brightness of the expanse of heaven; and those who turn many to righteousness, like the stars forever and ever. 4 But as for you, O Daniel, conceal these words and seal up the book until the time of the end; many will go to and fro,[48] and knowledge will increase."

---

44 Lit *truth*; Heb., *'emet*
45 I.e., keep the vision secret; Heb., *satar*
46 Lit *for to days many*; I.e., to the distant future
47 Lit make me understand
48 I.e. examine the book thoroughly

**Daniel 12:9-10** Updated American Standard Version (UASV)

⁹He said, "Go your way, Daniel, for the words are shut up and sealed until the time of the end. ¹⁰Many shall purify themselves and make themselves white and be refined, but the wicked shall act wickedly. And none of the wicked shall understand, but those who are wise shall understand.

**2 Corinthians 4:3-4** Updated American Standard Version (UASV)

³ And even if our gospel is veiled, it is veiled to those who are perishing. ⁴ In their case the god of this world has blinded the minds of the unbelievers, to keep them from seeing the light of the gospel of the glory of Christ, who is the image of God.

One of the principles of interpreting prophecy is to understand judgment prophecies. If a prophet declares judgment on a people, and they turn around from their bad course, the judgment may be lifted, which does not negate the trueness of the prophetic judgment message. There was simply a change in circumstances. There is a principle that most readers are not aware of:

**Jeremiah 18:7-8** Updated American Standard Version (UASV)

⁷ At one moment I might speak concerning a nation or concerning a kingdom to uproot, to tear down, and to destroy it; ⁸ and if that nation which I have spoken against turns from its evil, I will also feel regret over[49] the calamity that I intended to bring against it.

Another principle that needs to be understood is the language of prophecy. It uses imagery that is common to

------

[49] Lit repent of; .e., I will change my mind concerning; or I will think better of, or I will relent concerning

the people, with the exception of the highly apocalyptic literature. One form of imagery is the cosmic.

**Isaiah 13:9-11** Updated American Standard Version (UASV)

⁹ Behold, the day of Jehovah is coming,
    cruel, with wrath and burning anger,
to make the land a desolation;
    and he will destroy its sinners from it.
¹⁰ For the stars of the heavens and their constellations
    will not flash forth their light;
the sun will be dark when it rises,
    and the moon will not shed its light.
¹¹ And I will punish the world for its evil,
    and the wicked for their iniquity;
I will put an end to the arrogance of the proud,
    and lay low the haughtiness of tyrants.

It is often assumed that this sort of imagery is talking about the end of the world, and this is not always the case. Using Isaiah 13 as our example, it is talking about a pronouncement against Babylon, not the end of the world, as can be seen in verse 1. This type of terminology is a way of expressing that God is acting in behalf of man. At times, figurative language can come across as contradicting for the modern-day reader. For example, in chapter 21 of Revelation the walls of Jerusalem are described as being 200 feet thick. The walls are an image of safety and security for the New Jerusalem. However, in verse 25 we read that the gates are never shut. This immediate leads to the question of why have walls that cannot be penetrated, and then leave the gates open? Moreover, if gates are the weakest point to defend, why have twelve of them (vs. 12)? To the modern militaristic mind, this comes off as contradictory, but not to the Jewish-Christian mind of the first-century. Both present the picture of safety. It is so safe that you can leave the gates open. What about the idea of a "fuller meaning" that the prophet was not aware of? As we saw in the above, there would be symbolism meant for a day far into the future, but generally speaking, most prophets proclaimed a message that was applicable to their day, and implications for another day. Dr. Robert Stein addresses this issue:

> There are times when a prophetic text appears to have a fulfillment other than what the prophet himself apparently expected. (The following are frequently given as examples: Matt. 1:22–23; 2:15, 17–18; John 12:15; 1 Cor. 10:3–4.) Is it possible that a prophecy may have a deeper meaning or "fuller" sense than the prophet envisioned? . . . Rather than appealing to a "fuller sense" distinct and different from that of the biblical author, however, it may be wiser to see if the supposed *sensus plenior* is in reality an implication of the author's conscious meaning. Thus, when Paul in 1 Corinthians 9:9 quotes Deuteronomy 25:4 ("do not muzzle an ox while it is treading out the grain") as a justification for ministers of the gospel living off the gospel, this is not a "fuller" meaning of the text unrelated to what the author sought to convey. Rather, it is a legitimate implication of the willed pattern of meaning contained in Deuteronomy 25:4. If as a principle animals should be allowed to share in the benefits of their work, how much more should the "animal" who is made in the image of God and proclaims the Word of God be allowed to share in the benefits of that work! Thus, what Paul is saying is not a fuller and different meaning from what the writer of Deuteronomy meant. On the contrary, although this specific implication was unknown to him, it is part of his conscious and willed pattern of meaning. Perhaps such prophecies as Matthew 1:22–23 and 2:15 are best understood as revealing implications of the

original prophecies in Isaiah 7:14 and Hosea 11:1. Whereas in Isaiah's day the prophet meant that a maiden would give birth to a son who was named "Immanuel," that willed meaning also allows for a virgin one day to give birth to a son who would be Immanuel. Whereas God showed his covenantal faithfulness by leading his "son," his children, back from Egypt to the promised land in Moses' day so also did he lead his "Son," Jesus, back from Egypt to the promised land. [50]

Getting back to Daniel, we can clearly see that his book is prophetic and the only Old Testament apocalyptic book at that, which makes him a special target for the Bible critic. The critic has deemed that Daniel did not pen the book that bears his name, but another writer penned the words some centuries later.[51] These attacks have become such a reality that most scholars accept the late date of 165 B.C.E., by a pseudonym. As we have learned throughout this book, it is never the majority that establishes something as being true, simply for the fact of being the majority; it is the evidence. If the evidence proves that Daniel did not write the book, then the words are meaningless, and the hope that it contains is not there.

For example, take the allegation made in *The Encyclopedia Americana*: "Many historical details of the earlier periods [such as that of the Babylonian exile] have been badly garbled" in Daniel. Really? We will take up three of those alleged mistakes.

---

[50] Robert H. Stein, *A Basic Guide to Interpreting the Bible: Playing by the Rules* (Grand Rapids, MI: Baker Books, 1994), 97.

[51] Some Bible critics attempt to lessen the charge of forgery by saying that the writer used Daniel as a false name (pseudonym), just as some ancient noncanonical books were written under assumed names. In spite of this, the Bible critic Ferdinand Hitzig held: "The case of the book of Daniel, if it is assigned to any other [writer], is different. Then it becomes a forged writing, and the intention was to deceive his immediate readers, though for their good."

# Claims That Belshazzar Is Missing From History

**Daniel 5:1, 11, 18, 22, 30** Updated American Standard Version (UASV)

¹ Belshazzar the king made[52] a great feast for a thousand of his nobles, and he was drinking wine in the presence of the thousand.

¹¹ There is a man in your kingdom in whom is a spirit of the holy gods;[53] and in the days of your father, enlightenment, insight, and wisdom like the wisdom of the gods were found in him. And King Nebuchadnezzar, your father, your father the king, appointed him chief of the magic-practicing priests, conjurers, Chaldeans and diviners.

¹⁸ You. O king, the Most High God granted the kingdom and the greatness and the glory and the majesty to Nebuchadnezzar your father.

²² "But you, his son[54] Belshazzar, have not humbled your heart, although you knew all of this,

³⁰ That same night Belshazzar the Chaldean king was killed.

In 1850 German scholar Ferdinand Hitzig said in a commentary on the book of Daniel, confidently declaring that Belshazzar was "a figment of the writer's imagination."[55] His reasoning was that Daniel was missing from history, only found in the book of Daniel itself. Does this not seem a bit premature? Is it so irrational to think that a person might not be readily located by archaeology, a brand new field at the time, especially from a period that

---

[52] I.e., held
[53] Spirit of ... gods Aram., ruach-'elahin'; Or possibly the Spirit of the holy God
[54] Or descendant
[55] *Das Buch Daniel.* Ferdinand Hitzig. Weidman (Leipzig) 1850.

was yet to be fully explored? Regardless, in 1854, there was a discovery of some small cylinders in the ancient city of Babylon and Ur, southern Iraq. The cuneiform documents were from King Nabonidus, and they included a prayer for "Belshazzar my firstborn son, the offspring of my heart." This discovery was a mere four years after Hitzig made his rash judgment.

Of course, not all critics would be satisfied. H. F. Talbot made the statement, "This proves nothing." The charge by Talbot was that Belshazzar was likely a mere child, but Daniel has him as being king. Well, this critical remark did not even stay alive as long as Hitzig's had. Within the year, more cuneiform tablets were discovered, this time they stated he had secretaries, as well as a household staff. Obviously, Belshazzar was not a child! However, more was to come, as other tablets explained that Belshazzar was a coregent king while Nabonidus was away from Babylon for years at a time.[56]

One would think that the critic might concede. Still disgruntled, some argued that the Bible calls Belshazzar, the son of Nebuchadnezzar, and not the son of Nabonidus. Others comment that Daniel nowhere mentions the name of Nabonidus. Once again, both arguments are dismantled with a deeper observation. Nabonidus married the daughter of Nebuchadnezzar, making Belshazzar the grandson of Nebuchadnezzar. Both Hebrew and Aramaic language do not have words for "grandfather" or "grandson"; "son of" also means "grandson of" or even "descendant of." (See Matthew 1:1.) Moreover, the account in Daniel does infer that Belshazzar is the son of Nabonidus. When the mysterious handwriting was on the wall, the horrified Belshazzar offered the *third*

---

[56] When Babylon fell, Nabonidus was away. Therefore, Daniel was correct in that Belshazzar was the king at that time. Critics still try to cling to their Bible difficulty by stating that no secular records state that Belshazzar was a king. When will they quit with this quibbling? Even governors in the Ancient Near East were stated as being kings at times.

place in his kingdom, to whoever could interpret it. (Daniel 5:7) The observant reader will notice that Nabonidus held first place in the kingdom, while Daniel held the second place, leaving the third place for the interpreter.

## Darius the Mede

One would think that the critic would have learned his lesson from Belshazzar. However, this is just not the case. Daniel 5:31 reads: "and Darius the Mede received the kingdom, being about sixty-two years old." Here again, the critical scholar argues that Darius does not exist, as he has never been found in secular or archaeological records. Therefore, *The New Encyclopædia Britannica* declares that this Darius is "a fictitious character."

There is no doubt that in time; Darius will be unearthed by archaeology, just as Belshazzar has. There is initial information that allows for inferences already. Cuneiform tablets have been discovered that shows Cyrus the Persian did not take over as the "King of Babylon" directly after the conquest. Rather he carried the title "King of the Lands."[57] W. H Shea suggests, "Whoever bore the title of 'King of Babylon' was a vassal king under Cyrus, not Cyrus himself." Is it possible that Darius is simply a title of a person that was placed in charge of Babylon? Some scholars suggest a man named Gubaru was the real Darius. Secular records do show that Cyrus appointed Gubaru as governor over Babylon, giving him considerable power. Looking to the cuneiform tablets again, we find that Cyrus appointed subgovernors over Babylon. Fascinatingly, Daniel notes that Darius selected 120 satraps to oversee the kingdom of Babylon.—Daniel 6:1.

---

[57] This evidence is found in royal titles in economic texts, which just so happens to date to the first two years of Cyrus' rule.

EDWARD D. ANDREWS

We should realize that archaeology is continuously bringing unknown people to light all the time, and in time, it may shed more light on Darius. However, for now, and based on the fact that many Bible characters have been established, it is a little ridiculous to consider Darius as "fictitious," worse still to view the whole of the book of Daniel as a fraud. In fact, it is best to see Daniel as a person, who was right there in the midst of that history, giving him access to more court records.

After Belshazzar (King of Babylon), Sargon (Assyrian Monarch), and the like have been assailed with being nonexistent, the Bible critic and liberal scholars do the same with Darius the Mede, and Mordecai in the book of Esther. This illustrates the folly of assigning boundless confidence in the ancient secular records, while we wait in secular sources to validate Scripture. Most outside of true conservative Christianity carries the presupposition that the Bible is a myth, legend and erroneous until secular sources support it.

Bible critics argued profusely that Belshazzar was not a historical person. Then, evidence came in that substantiated Belshazzar, and the Bible critic just moves on to another like Sargon, saying that he was not a real historical person, as though they had never raised such an objection for Belshazzar. Then, evidence came in that substantiated Sargon, and the Bible critic would silently move on yet again. This is repeated time after time.

The Bible critics, liberal and moderate Bible scholars believe the Bible is wrong until validated by secular history. They move the goal post of trustworthiness as they please so that Scripture will never be authentic and true, it will never be trustworthy, and to these ones, it is not the inspired, fully inerrant Word of God, as far as they are concerned.

Why do we continue to cater to these ones, as though we need to appease them somehow?

# King Jehoiakim

**Daniel 1:1** Updated American Standard Version (UASV)

¹ In the third year of the reign of Jehoiakim king of Judah, Nebuchadnezzar king of Babylon came to Jerusalem and besieged it.

**Jeremiah 25:1** Updated American Standard Version (UASV)

¹ The word that came to Jeremiah concerning all the people of Judah, in the fourth year of Jehoiakim the son of Josiah, king of Judah (that was the first year of Nebuchadnezzar king of Babylon),

**Jeremiah 46:2** Updated American Standard Version (UASV)

² About Egypt, concerning the army of Pharaoh Neco king of Egypt, which was by the Euphrates River at Carchemish, which Nebuchadnezzar king of Babylon defeated in the fourth year of Jehoiakim, the son of Josiah, king of Judah:

The Bible critic finds fault with Daniel 1:1 as it is not in harmony with Jeremiah, who says "in the fourth year of Jehoiakim, the son of Josiah, king of Judah (that was the first year of Nebuchadnezzar king of Babylon)." The Bible student who looks a little deeper will find that there is really no contradiction at all. Pharaoh Necho first made Jehoiakim king in 628 B.C.E. Three years would pass before Nebuchadnezzar succeeded his father as King in Babylon, in 624 B.C.E. In 620 B.C.E., Nebuchadnezzar conquered Judah and made Jehoiakim the subordinate king under Babylon. (2 Kings 23:34; 24:1) Therefore, it is all about the perspective of the writer and where he was when penning his book. Daniel wrote from Babylon; therefore, Jehoiakim's third year would have been when he was made a subordinate king to Babylon. Jeremiah on the other hand wrote from Jerusalem, so he is referring to the time when Jehoiakim was made a subordinate king under Pharaoh Necho.

This so-called discrepancy really just adds more weight to the fact that it was Daniel, who penned the book bearing his name. In addition, it must be remembered that Daniel had Jeremiah's book with him. (Daniel 9:2) Therefore, are we to believe that Daniel was this clever forger, and at the same time, he would contradict the well-known book of Jeremiah, especially in verse 1?

## Positive Details

There are many details in the book of Daniel itself, which give credence to its authenticity. For example, Daniel 3:1-6 tells us that Nebuchadnezzar set up a huge image of gold, which his people were to worship. Archaeology has found evidence that credits Nebuchadnezzar with attempts to involve the people more in nationalistic and religious practices. Likewise, Daniel addresses Nebuchadnezzar's arrogant attitude about his many construction plans. (Daniel 4:30) It is not until modern-day archaeology uncovered evidence that we now know Nebuchadnezzar was the person who built much of Babylon. Moreover, his boastful attitude is made quite evident by having his name stamped on the bricks. This fact would not have been something a forger from 167-63 B.C.E. would have known about because the bricks hadn't at that time been unearthed.

The writer of Daniel was very familiar with the differences between Babylonian and Medo-Persian law. The three friends of Daniel were thrown into the fiery furnace for disobeying the Babylonian law, while Daniel, decades later under Persian law, was thrown into a lion's pit for violating the law. (Daniel 3:6; 6:7-9) Archaeology has again proven to be a great help, for they have uncovered an actual letter that shows the fiery furnace was a form of punishment. However, the Medes and Persians would not have used this form of punishment; as fire was sacred to them. Thus, they had other forms of capital punishment.

Another piece of inside knowledge is that Nebuchadnezzar passed and changed laws as he pleased. Darius, on the other hand, was unable to change a law once it was passed, even one that he himself had commissioned. (Daniel 2:5, 6, 24, 46-49; 3:10, 11, 29; 6:12-16) Historian John C. Whitcomb writes: "Ancient history substantiates this difference between Babylon, where the law was subject to the king, and Medo-Persia, where the king was subject to the law."

**Daniel 5:1-4** Updated American Standard Version (UASV)

¹ Belshazzar the king made[58] a great feast for a thousand of his nobles, and he was drinking wine in the presence of the thousand.

² Belshazzar, when he tasted the wine, commanded that the vessels of gold and of silver that Nebuchadnezzar his father[59] had taken out of the temple in Jerusalem be brought, that the king and his nobles, his wives, and his concubines might drink from them. ³ Then they brought the gold vessels that had been taken out of the temple, the house of God which was in Jerusalem; and the king and his nobles, his wives and his concubines drank from them. ⁴ They drank the wine and praised the gods of gold and silver, of bronze, iron, wood and stone.

Archaeology has substantiated these kinds of feasts. The fact that stands out is the mention of women being present at the feast, the "wives, and his concubines" were

---

[58] I.e., held
[59] Or *predecessor*; also verses 11, 13, 18

present as well. Such an idea would have been repugnant to the Greeks and Jews of 167-67 B.C.E. era. This may very well be why the Greek Septuagint version of Daniel removed the mention of these women.[60] This so-called forger of Daniel would have live during this same time of the Septuagint.

## Do External Factors Prove Daniel Is A Forgery?

Even the place of Daniel in the canon of the Hebrew Old Testament is evidence against his having written the book, so says the critics. The Jewish scribes (like Ezra) of ancient Israel arranged the books of the Old Testament into three groups: the Torah, the Prophets, and the Writings. Naturally, we would expect that Daniel would be found among the Prophets, yet they placed him among the Writings. Therefore, the critic makes the argument that Daniel had to of been an unknown when the works of the prophets were being collected. Their theory is that it was placed among the writings because these were collected last.

However, not all Bible scholarship agree that the ancient scribes placed Daniel in the Writings, and not the Prophets. However, even if it is as they claim, Daniel was added among the Writings; this does nothing to prove that it was penned at a later date. Old Testament Bible scholar Gleason L. Archer states that . . .

> It should be noted that some of the documents in the Kethubhim [Writings] (the third division of the Hebrew Bible) were of great antiquity, such as the book of Job, the Davidic psalms, and the writings of Solomon. Position in the Kethubhim, therefore, is no proof of a late

---

[60] Hebrew scholar C. F. Keil writes of Daniel 5:3: "The LXX. have here, and also at ver. 23, omitted mention of the women, according to the custom of the Macedonians, Greeks, and Romans."

date of composition. Furthermore the statement in Josephus (Contra Apionem. 1:8) quoted previously in chapter 5 indicates strongly that in the first century A.D., Daniel was included among the prophets in the second division of the Old Testament canon; hence it could not have been assigned to the Kethubim until a later period. 349 The Masoretes may have been influenced in this reassignment by the consideration that Daniel was not appointed or ordained as a prophet, but remained a civil servant under the prevailing government throughout his entire career. Second, a large percentage of his writings does not bear the character of prophecy, but rather of history (chaps. 1-6), such as does not appear in any of the books of the canonical prophets.350 Little of that which Daniel wrote is couched in the form of a message from God to His people relayed through the mouth of His spokesman. Rather, the predominating element consists of prophetic visions granted personally to the author and interpreted to him by angels.[61]

The critic also turns his attention to the Apocryphal book, Ecclesiasticus, by Jesus Ben Sirach, penned about 180 B.C.E., as evidence that Daniel did not pen the book that bears his name. Ecclesiasticus has a long list of righteous men, of which, Daniel is missing. From this, they conclude that Daniel had to of been an unknown at the time. However, if we follow that line of reasoning; what do we do with the fact that the same list omits: Ezra and Mordecai, good King Jehoshaphat, and the upright man Job; of all the judges, except Samuel.[62] Simply because the

---

[61] Archer, Gleason (1996-08-01). A Survey of Old Testament Introduction (Kindle Locations 7963-7972). Moody Publishers.

[62] If we turn our attention to the Apostle Paul's list of faithful men and women found in Hebrews chapter 11; it does appear to mention

above faithful and righteous men are missing from a list in an apocryphal book, are we to dismiss them as having never existed? The very idea is absurd.

## Sources in Favor of Daniel

Ezekiel's references to Daniel must be considered to be one of the strongest arguments for a sixth-century date. No satisfactory explanation exists for the use of the name Daniel by the prophet Ezekiel other than that he and Daniel were contemporaries and that Daniel had already become widely known throughout the Babylonian Empire by the time of Ezekiel's ministry.[63]

We have in chapter 9 a series of remarkable predictions which defy any other interpretation but that they point to the coming of Christ and His crucifixion [about] A.D. 30, followed by the destruction of the city of Jerusalem within the ensuing decades. In Dan. 9:25–26, it is stated that sixty-nine heptads of years (i.e., 483 years) will ensue between a "decree" to rebuild the walls of Jerusalem, and the cutting off of Messiah the Prince. In 9:25–26, we read: "Know therefore and understand, that from the going forth of the commandment to restore and to build Jerusalem unto the Messiah the Prince shall be seven weeks, and threescore and two weeks.... And after threescore and two weeks shall Messiah be cut off, but not for himself: and

---

occasions recorded in Daniel. (Daniel 6:16-24; Hebrews 11:32, 33) Nevertheless, the list by Paul is not an exhaustive list either. Even within his list, Isaiah, Jeremiah, and Ezekiel are not named in the list, but this scarcely demonstrates that they never existed.

63 Stephen R. Miller, vol. 18, *Daniel*, electronic ed., Logos Library System; The New American Commentary (Nashville: Broadman & Holman Publishers, 2001), 42-43.

the people of the prince that shall come shall destroy the city and the sanctuary."[64]

## The Greatest Evidence for Daniel

First of all, we have the clear testimony of the Lord Jesus Himself in the Olivet discourse. In Matt. 24:15, He refers to "the abomination of desolation, spoken of through [*dia*] Daniel the prophet." The phrase "abomination of desolation" occurs three times in Daniel (9:27; 11:31; 12:11). If these words of Christ are reliably reported, we can only conclude that He believed the historic Daniel to be the personal author of the prophecies containing this phrase. No other interpretation is possible in the light of the preposition *dia*, which refers to personal agency. It is significant that Jesus regarded this "abomination" as something to be brought to pass in a future age rather than being simply the idol of Zeus set up by Antiochus in the temple, as the Maccabean theorists insist.[65]

While this has certainly been an overview of the evidence in favor of the authenticity of Daniel, there will never be enough to satisfy the critic. One professor at Oxford University wrote: "Nothing is gained by a mere answer to objections, so long as the original prejudice, 'there cannot be supernatural prophecy,' remains." What does this mean? It means that the critic is blinded by his prejudice. However, God has given them the choice of free will.

---

[64] Gleason Leonard Archer, *A Survey of Old Testament Introduction*, 3rd. ed.]. (Chicago: Moody Press, 1998), 445.

[65] Gleason Leonard Archer, *A Survey of Old Testament Introduction*, 3rd. ed.]. (Chicago: Moody Press, 1998), 444.

The Bible critics are ever so vigilant today in their efforts to undermine the Word of God. They are more prepared than most Christians and witness about their doubts far more than your average Christian witnesses about his or her faith.

**1 Peter 3:15** Updated American Standard Version (UASV)

[15] but sanctify Christ as Lord in your hearts, always being prepared to make a defense[66] to anyone who asks you for a reason for the hope that is in you; yet do it with gentleness and respect;

Peter says that we must be prepared to make a *defense*. The Greek word behind the English "defense" is *apologia* (apologia), which is actually a legal term that refers to the defense of a defendant in court. Our English apologetics is just what Peter spoke of, having the ability to give a reason to any who may challenge us or to answer those who are not challenging us but who have honest questions that deserve to be answered.

To whom was the apostle Peter talking? Whom was Peter saying needed always to be prepared to make a defense? Was he talking only to the pastors, elders, servants, or was he speaking to all Christians? Peter opens this letter saying, "to the chosen who are residing temporarily in the dispersion in Pontus, Galatia, Cappadocia, Asia, and Bithynia." Who are these "chosen" ones? The College Press NIV Commentary gives us the answer,

The Greek text does not include the word "God's," but the translation is a fair one since the clear implication is that God did the choosing. The word Peter uses has a rich biblical heritage. The Jews found their identity and the basis of their lives in the fact that they were God's chosen people (see, e.g., Deut 7:6–8). The New Testament

---

[66] Or argument; or explanation

frequently identifies Christians as elect or chosen. In 1 Peter 2:9 Peter will identify Christians as "a chosen people," using the same word ἐκλεκτός (*eklektos*) here translated "elect." The same word is also used of Christ in 2:4 and 6 (where it is translated "chosen"). Christians are chosen or elect through the chosen or elect One, Jesus Christ. The idea that Christians are God's chosen people is fundamental to Peter's thinking, as is apparent in 1:13–2:10. Peter is already laying the foundation for his appeals to these Christians to live up to their holy calling. (Black and Black 1998)

The "chosen who are residing temporarily in the dispersion" were Christians, who were living among non-Christian Jews and Gentiles. This letter, then, is addressed to all Christians, but the context of chapters 1:3 to 4:11 is mostly addressed to newly baptized Christians. Therefore, all Christians are obligated to 'be prepared to make a defense to anyone who asks us for a reason for the hope that is in us.' Yes, we are all required to defend our hope successfully. If any have not felt they were up to the task, this author by way of Christian publishing House are publishing books to help along those lines. Here is what is available at present, including this publication you are reading,

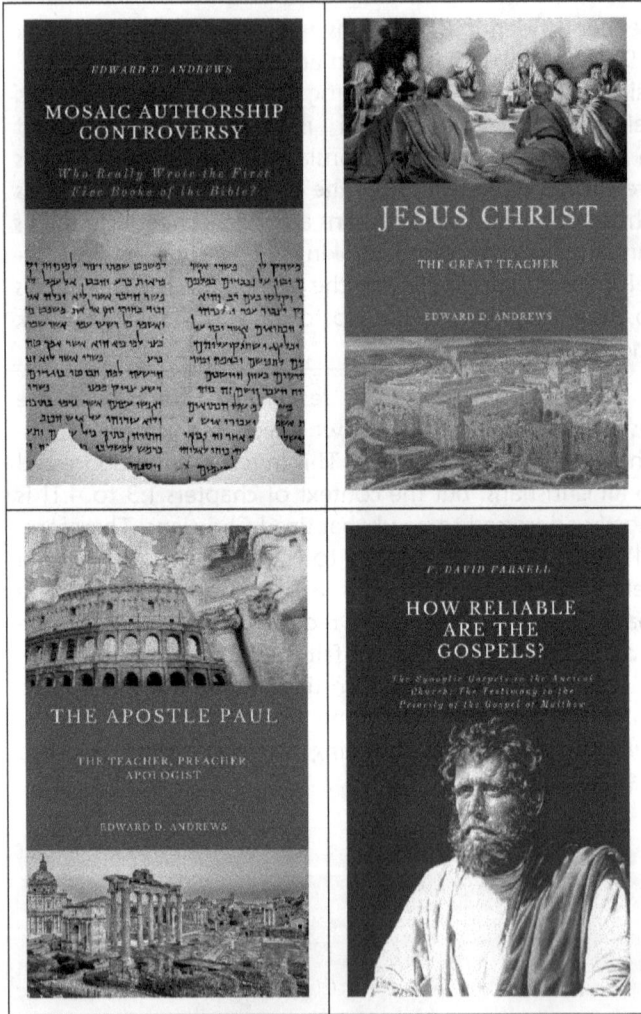

These first-century Christians in Asia Minor were in a time of difficulty. They were at the time of Peter's letter; about 62-64 C.E. going through some trials, not knowing that many far more severe lie in the not too distant future. Within a few years, the persecution of Christians by Emperor Nero would begin. These new converts had given up former religions, idols, cults and superstitions, their 'the futile ways inherited from your forefathers.' (1 Pet. 1:18) These ones were taking off their old person, and bringing their lives in harmony with God's Word, such as 'malice and deceit and hypocrisy and envy and slander.' (1 Pet. 2:1) Now they were 'no longer living for the lusts of men, but for the will of God.' (1 Pet. 4:2) Their former pagan friends now hated these new Christians, because 'they were surprised when these chosen ones do not join them in the same flood of debauchery, and they maligned them.' (1 Pet. 4:4) In fact, Peter informs us that Satan, the Devil is enraged when one is converted from their former life of debauchery, conformed instead to the Word of God. Peter warned them, "Be sober-minded; be watchful. Your adversary the devil prowls around like a roaring lion, seeking someone to devour." 1 Peter 5:8

Christians have never really had it easy in defending their hope. Peter counsels these new ones, who have next to no experience in coping with trials and persecutions to rejoice, albeit distressed by numerous trials. "**Keep your conduct among the Gentiles honorable**, so that when they speak against you as evildoers, they may see your good deeds and glorify God on the day of visitation." (1 Pet. 2:12) "The end of all things is at hand; therefore **be self-controlled and sober-minded for the sake of your prayers.**" 1 Pet. 4:4) "Be sober-minded; be watchful" in the midst of men who continue "living in sensuality, passions, drunkenness, orgies, drinking parties, and lawless idolatry." (1 Pet. 4:3) They should be united under Christ as they 'Have purified their souls by their obedience to the truth for a sincere brotherly love, love one another earnestly from a pure heart." (1 Peter 1:22) "Above all, [they were to] keep loving one another earnestly, since love covers a multitude of sins. Show hospitality to one another without grumbling. As each has received a gift, use it to serve one another, as good stewards of God's varied grace." (1 Pet 4:8-10) 'Finally, all of them, had unity of mind, sympathy, brotherly love, a tender heart, and a humble mind. They did not repay evil for evil or reviling for reviling, but on the contrary, they blessed, for to this they were called, that you may obtain a blessing.' (1 Pet. 3:8-9) If they heeded this counsel, it would have kept them from falling or drifting back into their former ways.

There was one more obligation if they were to preserve on the right path of conduct, namely, being prepared to make a defense for their hope. "It was revealed to [the prophets] that they were serving not themselves but you, in the things that have now been announced to you through those who preached the good news to you by the Holy Spirit sent from heaven, things into which angels long to look. Therefore, preparing your minds for action, and being sober-minded, set your hope fully on the grace that will be brought to you at the revelation of Jesus Christ." (1 Pet. 1:12-13) Peter went on to tell them that they were "a chosen race, a royal priesthood, a holy nation, a people for his own possession, that you may proclaim the excellencies of him who called you out of darkness into his marvelous light." (1 Pet. 2:9) When should they "proclaim these excellencies"? He writes, "but in your hearts honor Christ the Lord as holy, **always** **being prepared** to make a defense to anyone who asks you for a reason for the hope that is in you; yet do it with gentleness and respect." 1 Peter 3:15

The world in which we live today is much vaster than that of the first-century up unto the 21st-century. The trials and persecution today are much more intense, which unfortunately we ca watch around the world, by way of the media and social media. The greatest threat to Christianity is Islam, which has been an ardent enemy of Christianity since the seventh-century C.E. They are slaughtering Christians the world over. They view Christians as the big Satan and the Jews as little Satan. In their theology, they are looking to turn the world into one big Islamic state, governed by the Quran. For the more radical aspects of Islam, it is convert to Islam or be killed as an infidel.

The second greatest threat to tradition and conservatism is liberal Christianity. Their continued dissecting of the Scriptures until Moses did not pen the first five books, Isaiah is not the author of the book that bears his name, nor is Daniel the author of the book that bears his name, and the Bible is full of myths and legends, errors and contractions.

Then, as we have seen throughout this publication, there are moderate and liberal Bible scholars, who are advocates of Historical Criticism Methodology, and its sub-criticisms: Source Criticism, Tradition Criticism, Form Criticism, Redaction Criticism, among others.

**2 Timothy 2:24-25** Updated American Standard Version (ASV)

[24] For a slave of the Lord does not need to fight, but needs to be kind to all, qualified to teach, showing restraint when wronged, [25] instructing his opponents with gentleness, if perhaps God may grant them repentance leading to accurate knowledge [*epignosis*][67] of the truth,

Look at the Greek word (*epignosis*) behind the English "knowledge" from above. "It is more intensive than *gnosis*, knowledge because it expresses a more thorough participation in the acquiring of knowledge on the part of the learner."[68] The requirement of all of the Lord's servants is that they be able to teach, but not in a

---

[67] *Epignosis* is a strengthened or intensified form of *gnosis* (*epi*, meaning "additional"), meaning, "true," "real," "full," "complete" or "accurate," depending upon the context. Paul and Peter alone use *epignosis*.

68. Spiros Zodhiates, *The Complete Word Study Dictionary: New Testament*, Electronic ed. (Chattanooga, TN: AMG Publishers, 2000, c1992, c1993), S. G1922.

quarrelsome way, but in a way to correct opponents with mildness. Why? The purpose of it all is that by God, yet through the Christian teacher, one may come to repentance and begin taking in an accurate knowledge of the truth.

> Some Christians see apologetics as pre-evangelism; it is not the gospel, but it prepares the soil for the gospel.[69] Others make no such distinction, seeing apologetics, theology, philosophy, and evangelism as deeply entwined facets of the gospel.[70] Whatever its relation to the gospel, apologetics **is an extremely important enterprise that can profoundly impact unbelievers** and be used as the tool that clears the way to faith in Jesus Christ. (Bold mine.)

> Many Christians did not come to believe as a result of investigating the Bible's authority, the evidence for the resurrection, or as a response to the philosophical arguments for God's existence. They responded to the proclamation of the gospel. Although these people have reasons for their belief, they are deeply personal reasons that often do not make sense to unbelievers. **They know the truth but are not necessarily equipped to share or articulate the truth in a way that is understandable** to those who have questions about their faith. It is quite possible to believe something is true without having a proper understanding of it or the ability to articulate it. (Bold mine.)

> Christians who believe but do not know why are often insecure and comfortable only around other Christians. Defensiveness can

---

[69] Norman Geisler and Ron Brooks, When Skeptics Ask (Grand Rapids: Baker Books, 1996), 11.

[70] Greg Bahnsen, Van Til Apologetic (Phillipsburg, NJ: Presbyterian and Reformed, 1998), 43.

quickly surface when challenges arise on issues of faith, morality, and truth because of a lack of information regarding the rational grounds for Christianity. At its worst, this can lead to either a fortress mentality or a belligerent faith, precisely the opposite of the Great Commission Jesus gave in Matthew 28:19–20. The Christian's charge is not to withdraw from the world and lead an insular life. Rather, we must be engaged in the culture, to be salt and light.

The solution to this problem requires believers to become informed in doctrine, the history of their faith, philosophy, logic, and other disciplines as they relate to Christianity. Believers must know the facts, arguments and theology and understand how to employ them in a way that will effectively engage the culture. Believers need Christian apologetics. One of the first tasks of Christian apologetics provides information. A number of widely held assumptions about Christianity can be easily challenged with a little information. This is even true for persons who are generally well-educated.[71]

The ability to reason with others will take time, practice and patience. For example, if someone reasons with others successfully, that person must be reasonable. In a discussion about the historicity about Jesus, a believer knows the other person denying the existence of Jesus is wrong. Moreover, believers possess a truckload of evidence to support this position. However, it is best sometimes to not unload the truck by dumping the entire load at a listener's feet in one conversation, or in one

---

[71] Powell, Doug (2006-07-01). *Holman QuickSource Guide to Christian Apologetics* (Holman Quicksource Guides) (p. 6-7). B&H Publishing. Kindle Edition.

breath. Being reasonable does not mean that a believer compromises the truth because he or she does not unload on the listener.

The other person will likely make many wrong statements in the conversation, and we should let most of them go unchallenged; rather, focus on a handful of the most crucial pieces of evidence and do not get lost by refuting every wrong statement. He may make bold condemnatory statements about many Christian beliefs, but we need to remain calm and not make a big deal of those statements. Listen carefully to the other person, and stay within the boundaries of the evidence in the conversation. For example, in a conversation on the historicity of Jesus when the listener states, "The New Testament manuscripts were completely corrupted in the copying process for a millennium, to the point that we do not even have the supposed Word of God." The evidence for the historicity of Jesus rests in the first and second century, so it would be a fool's errand to get into an extensive side subject about the restoration of the New Testament text, which took place over the centuries that followed the first two centuries C.E. There will be another day to talk about the history of the Greek New Testament, but today focus on the historicity of Jesus Christ.

God has given humanity free will, meaning each human has the right to choose, even if that choice is unwise. Believers have the assignment of proclaiming "the good news of the kingdom," as well as "making disciples" of redeemable humankind. Therefore, we must not pressure, coerce, or force people to accept the truth of that "Good News." However, all Christians have an obligation to reason with anyone by respectfully, gently, and mildly overturning their false reasoning, in the attempt that being used by God we may save some.

# Bibliography

Arnold, C. E. (2002). *Zondervan Illustrated Bible Backgrounds Commentary Volume 2: John, Acts.* . Grand Rapids, MI: Zondervan.

Barclay, W. (2002). *The Letter to the Hebrews (New Daily Study Bible).* Louisville, KY: Westminster John Knox Press.

Black, A., & Black, M. C. (1998). *THE COLLEGE PRESS NIV COMMENTARY 1 & 2 PETER.* Joplin: College Press Publishing Company.

Bruce, F. F. (1977). *Paul: Apostle of the Free Spirit.* Milton Keynes, UK: Paternoster.

Bruce, F. F. (1990). *The New International Commentary on the New Testament: The Epistle to the Hebrews (Revised).* Grand Rapids, MI: William B. Eermans Publishing Company.

Ellingworth, P. (1993). *The Epistle to the Hebrews: A Commentary on the Greek Text.* Grand Rapids, MI: W.B. Eerdmans.

Guthrie, G. H. (1998). *The NIV Application Commentary: Hebrews.* Grand Rapids, MI: Zondervan.

Kistemaker, S. J. (1984). *Baker New Testament Commentary: Hebrews.* Grand Rapids: Baker Books.

Lea, T. D. (1999). *Holman New Testament Commentary: Hebrews, James.* Nashville, TN: Broadman & Holman Publishers.

Outlaw, W. S. (2005). *The Book of Hebrews .* Nashville, TN: Randall House.

EDWARD D. ANDREWS

Pink, A. W. (1954). *An Exposition of Hebrews*. Swengel, PA: Bible Truth Depot.

Wright, N. T. (2003). *Hebrews for Everyone*. London: Westminster John Knox Press.

www.ingramcontent.com/pod-product-compliance
Lightning Source LLC
Chambersburg PA
CBHW060029050426
42448CB00012B/2912